# Political Corruption

by Debra A. Miller

**LUCENT BOOKS**

*An imprint of Thomson Gale, a part of The Thomson Corporation*

Detroit • New York • San Francisco • New Haven, Conn. • Waterville, Maine • London

LIBRARY OF CONGRESS CATALOGING-IN-PUBLICATION DATA

Miller, Debra A.
  Political corruption / by Debra A. Miller.
    p. cm.—(Hot topics)
  Includes bibliographical references and index.
  ISBN 978-1-59018-982-5 (hardcover)
  1. Political corruption—Juvenile literature. I. Title.
  JF1081.M55 2007
  364.1'323—dc22
                                                                2007007793

ISBN-10: 1-59018-982-5

Printed in the United States of America

# CONTENTS

6/12/08

# FOREWORD

Young people today are bombarded with information. Aside from traditional sources such as newspapers, television, and the radio, they are inundated with a nearly continuous stream of data from electronic media. They send and receive e-mails and instant messages, read and write online "blogs," participate in chat rooms and forums, and surf the Web for hours. This trend is likely to continue. As Patricia Senn Breivik, the dean of university libraries at Wayne State University in Detroit, states, "Information overload will only increase in the future. By 2020, for example, the available body of information is expected to double every 73 days! How will these students find the information they need in this coming tidal wave of information?"

Ironically, this overabundance of information can actually impede efforts to understand complex issues. Whether the topic is abortion, the death penalty, gay rights, or obesity, the deluge of fact and opinion that floods the print and electronic media is overwhelming. The news media report the results of polls and studies that contradict one another. Cable news shows, talk radio programs, and newspaper editorials promote narrow viewpoints and omit facts that challenge their own political biases. The World Wide Web is an electronic minefield where legitimate scholars compete with the postings of ordinary citizens who may or may not be well-informed or capable of reasoned argument. At times, strongly worded testimonials and opinion pieces both in print and electronic media are presented as factual accounts.

Conflicting quotes and statistics can confuse even the most diligent researchers. A good example of this is the question of whether or not the death penalty deters crime. For instance, one study found that murders decreased by nearly one-third when the death penalty was reinstated in New York in 1995. Death penalty supporters cite this finding to support their argument that the existence of the death penalty deters criminals from committing murder. However, another study found that states without the death penalty have murder rates below the national average. This study is cited by opponents of capital punishment, who reject the claim that the death penalty deters murder. Students need context and clear, informed discussion if they are to think critically and make informed decisions.

The Hot Topics series is designed to help young people wade through the glut of fact, opinion, and rhetoric so that they can think critically about controversial issues. Only by reading and thinking critically will they be able to formulate a viewpoint that is not simply the parroted views of others. Each volume of the series focuses on one of today's most pressing social issues and provides a balanced overview of the topic. Carefully crafted narrative, fully documented primary and secondary source quotes, informative sidebars, and study questions all provide excellent starting points for research and discussion. Full-color photographs and charts enhance all volumes in the series. With its many useful features, the Hot Topics series is a valuable resource for young people struggling to understand the pressing issues of the modern era.

# INTRODUCTION

# A "CULTURE OF CORRUPTION?"

*P*olitical corruption—a term that encompasses everything from the occasional acceptance of illegal bribes by government officials to more subtle and systemic, or widespread, types of political influence—today is increasingly becoming a focus of great concern, both in the United States and in the international community. Hardly a new phenomenon, corruption has existed as long as governments have existed and has been present in the United States throughout its history. It is now seen by many experts as one of the biggest challenges for both developed and developing nations around the world. Highly sensationalized scandals involving illegal or improper behavior of prominent government officials and the cozy relationships between elected officials and wealthy corporations or other interests abound in local, national, and even international news. In 2006, for example, political corruption scandals filled the news in the United States. Three names in the news—Randy "Duke" Cunningham, Jack Abramoff, and Ken Lay—exemplify three different aspects of what many experts and commentators describe as a systemic "culture of corruption" in American politics.

The scandal involving longtime California Republican congressman Randy "Duke" Cunningham illustrates that, even today, blatant bribery has not been banished from U.S. politics. Ironically, Cunningham was a former Navy top gun pilot who had a reputation for patriotism and integrity. Yet he used his position on the House Intelligence and Appropriations committees to steer millions of dollars in defense contracts to firms in exchange for $2.4 million in bribes. One contractor bought Cunningham's San Diego house at an inflated price and provided him with a 42-foot yacht (13m) called the *Duke-Stir*. Other bribes included $1 million in checks, a two-hundred-thousand-dollar down payment on a condominium, and numerous other lavish gifts, such as oriental rugs, a Rolls-Royce, and a nineteenth-century Louis Philippe chest of drawers. In December 2005 Cunningham tearfully pled guilty to bribery and tax evasion and is serving an eight-year prison term.

The Jack Abramoff affair, meanwhile, was a high-profile lobbying scandal that provided damning evidence of the systemic problem of influence peddling in American democracy. Abramoff

*Randy "Duke" Cunningham, center, walks into the U.S. District Courthouse for sentencing after being convicted of conspiracy and tax evasion.*

was a former top aide to Texas Republican representative Tom DeLay who later became a big-time Washington lobbyist. Abramoff admitted to overcharging several Indian tribes around $80 million for lobbying activities and providing gifts and trips to public officials in exchange for favors. Campaign reports also showed hundreds of thousands of dollars in political contributions coming from Abramoff and his clients to prominent legislators. Abramoff pled guilty in January 2006 to three criminal felony counts of tax evasion and bribery and was sentenced to five years and ten months in prison and ordered to pay restitution of more than $21 million. Also convicted in the scandal were Abramoff's former lobbying partner, Michael Scanlon, as well as two former aides of powerful Republican House majority leader Tom DeLay. DeLay himself was indicted for illegal campaign finance activities in Texas and resigned from Congress in June 2006.

A third name, Ken Lay, represents another type of corruption—corporate fraud—that many critics say is the end result of a lack of government oversight bought by years of corporate campaign funds to high-level politicians. Lay was the chief executive officer of Enron, a huge energy company that imploded in a December 2001 bankruptcy that caused the loss of four thousand jobs, the end of millions of dollars' worth of employee pensions, and financial ruin for its many investors. Later, a Justice Department investigation found that Enron executives had engaged in a scheme of deception for years, lying about profits and concealing debts while selling off their own personal stock and generally defrauding employees and investors. In 2004, following a much-publicized trial, executive officers Ken Lay and Jeffrey Skilling were convicted on multiple counts of securities and wire fraud. Lay was awaiting sentencing when he died of a heart attack in July 2006. The Enron debacle, many commentators charge, would not have occurred if government officials, including those associated with the prominent George W. Bush family, had not repeatedly helped the company win favorable regulatory conditions and other government benefits while taking millions in company campaign contributions. These conditions, critics say, allowed Enron officials to reap huge profits and hide the company's financial weaknesses at the expense of consumers and stockholders.

*Ken Lay (right) with codefendant Jeffrey Skilling (walking up in the background) on their way into the federal courthouse during their fraud and conspiracy trial.*

Similar instances of outright bribery and influence over public officials also plague other countries, both rich and poor. In developing countries, widespread official corruption often diverts significant amounts of public funds into private hands, helping to perpetuate poverty, disease, and economic underdevelopment. With globalization and increasing trade among countries, corruption has only increased, sometimes reaching even into international organizations and programs. In many places, the public becomes overwhelmed by the seemingly endless parade of unethical and corrupt politicians and corporate executives and simply becomes apathetic about politics, concluding that corruption is entrenched in the political system and nothing can be done to stop it. The result, many experts say, is voter apathy, reflected in shockingly low voter turnouts, even in high-level national elections.

Various attempts have been made to root out corruption in politics, both in America and around the world. In the United States, early reforms resulted in fewer cases of bribery and similar forms of corruption that once were commonplace. Instead, a different problem of campaign finance corruption—involving uncontrolled amounts of corporate and special-interest money in political campaigns and the buying of political influence—has mushroomed to alarming proportions. Each attempt to legislate in this area, however, has been circumvented with new forms of corrupt behavior. The good news is that there appears to be a growing public opposition to corruption on all levels that is reflected in a number of local, national, and international movements for reform. Over time, with the help of committed leadership, a diligent press, and continuing anticorruption advocacy, corruption could one day become a rarity rather than a way of life.

# THE PROBLEM OF POLITICAL CORRUPTION

Political corruption takes various forms—small bribes, pay-offs, and kickbacks of money to government officials as well as much more serious, systemic types of corruption. Examples of systemic corruption include the high-level bribery and theft seen in many undeveloped countries and the campaign finance, lobbying, and corporate scandals that are often headline news in the United States. For most people, any level of political corruption is an obvious problem—a subversion of government's central purpose, which is to promote the public good. Indeed, most commentators and experts on the subject agree that political corruption is a significant threat to both basic democratic principles and economic development.

## Defining *Political Corruption*

In the broadest sense, corruption in politics involves misuse of public or government power for a private illegal or improper purpose—"the abuse of public office for private gain,"[1] to quote the definition used by the World Bank and the International Monetary Fund (IMF). Often, the improper purpose is to attain some form of private financial gain, such as personal wealth, increased business profits, or a less competitive or regulated business environment that might lead to greater corporate profits. A government official may take a bribe or steal public funds to pay off a gambling debt or enrich his or her own personal bank account. An individual or corporation might bribe a government official to argue or vote in favor of a policy that will help the company, or to encourage the government not to enforce a regulation that might be harmful to company profits.

Sometimes, however, money is not the object at all, and the goal of the improper activity is simply to attain greater political power or to achieve specific political ends considered important to a particular person or interest group. Political scandals come to mind, such as Watergate, which revealed that U.S. president Richard Nixon maintained a secret fund of illegal corporate donations that he used to spy on and discredit his political enemies. Nixon did not seek monetary enrichment; his purpose was to hold on to political power. In Watergate, as in most corruption cases, secrecy was paramount, because neither those giving the money nor the government officials involved want the illegal or improper arrangement to be known to the public, for fear of criminal prosecution, public scorn, or other negative consequences.

## CORRUPTION UNDERMINES DEMOCRACY

"Corruption is an insidious plague that . . . undermines democracy and the rule of law, leads to violations of human rights, distorts markets, erodes the quality of life and allows organized crime, terrorism and other threats to human security to flourish."
                                —UN secretary general Kofi Annan

Quoted in Barbara Crossette, "Corruption's Threat to Democracy," *Atlantic Online*, April 12, 2004. www.theatlantic.com/foreign/unwire/crossette2004-04-12.htm.

No matter what the motivation, the existence of political corruption—the purpose of which is to serve private interests—is often viewed as the opposite of good governance. Governance is a term used to refer to the system and institutions created by a government to provide for the common good of its citizens. As Steven P. Lanza, executive editor of the *Connecticut Economy Quarterly* magazine, puts it, "Public officials are supposed to be trustees of the commonwealth, not political buccaneers seeking their own private gain."[2]

## Democracy and Political Corruption

Experts say that all types of governments—both democracies and more authoritarian governments—are susceptible to the all-too-human elevation of self-interest over the public interest that lies at the heart of political corruption. Despite this fact, a common argument is that the establishment of democracy helps to reduce corruption in developing countries. Certainly it is true that democracies tend to be more open, with a greater number of restrictions on behaviors that could be considered corrupt. Conversely, nondemocratic and more authoritarian nations have fewer checks and balances on official actions and much more secrecy surrounding government processes. Yet democratic countries are hardly exempt from political corruption; the long string of political scandals in the United States is testimony to this fact. As Yale political scientist and corruption scholar Susan Rose-Ackerman succinctly puts it, "Clearly, democratic forms do not always succeed in checking corruption."[3]

# Notoriously Corrupt Leaders

According to the global watchdog group Transparency International, it is difficult to know for certain how much money has been embezzled by national leaders over the last two decades. However, the group lists the following nine leaders as some of the most notoriously corrupt and gives an estimate of the value of funds they embezzled:

| | | |
|---|---|---|
| Mohamed Suharto | President of Indonesia, 1967–98 | US $15-35 billion |
| Ferdinand Marcos | President of Philippines, 1972–86 | US $5-10 billion |
| Sani Abacha | President of Nigeria, 1993–98 | US $5 billion |
| Slobodan Milosevic | President of Serbia/Yugoslavia, 1989–2000 | US $ 1 billion |
| Jean-Claude Duvalier | President of Haiti, 1971–86 | US $ 300-800 million |
| Alberto Fujimori | President of Peru, 1990–2000 | US $ 600 million |
| Pavlo Lazarenko | Prime Minister of Ukraine, 1996–97 | US $114-200 million |
| Arnoldo Alemán | President of Nicaragua, 1997–2002 | US $ 100 million |
| Joseph Estrada | President of Philippines, 1998–2001 | US $ 78-80 million |

Robin Hodess, "Part One: Political Corruption," Transparency International, July 1, 2004. www.onlinewomenin politics.org/resources/0204_ti_corrupt.pdf.

At the same time, Rose-Ackerman argues that the stronger the democracy, the lower the likelihood of corruption. If a democracy, for example, has strong checks and balances and a clear separation of powers, such as the three separate and independent parts of government in the U.S. system (the legislative, judicial, and executive), there is less concentration of power in one government entity. Theoretically, this makes it more difficult for individuals or groups wishing to influence government through corruption to succeed, because success in corrupting any one part can be checked by the actions of the other branches of government.

## OPERATING WITH LITTLE CONCERN

"[Corruption] is a symptom that the political system is operating with little concern for the broader public interest."
—Susan Rose-Ackerman, professor of law and political science at Yale University and codirector of the Yale Law School's Center for Law, Economics, and Public Policy

Susan Rose-Ackerman, *Government and Corruption: Causes, Consequences, and Reform.* New York: Cambridge University Press, 1999, p. 226.

The degree of openness and accountability, often called transparency, built into the democratic system is also important, experts say. If the public has access to information that can reveal possibly corrupt influences on government, whether through government auditing and record-keeping systems or through information publicized by an independent press or private interest groups, citizens and voters can act as yet another check on government corruption. As a guide produced for developing countries by the United Nations (UN) Development Programme says, "Corruption is principally a governance issue —a failure of institutions and a lack of capacity to manage society by means of a framework of social, judicial, political and economic checks and balances."[4]

## Direct Forms of Political Corruption

The most easily recognized types of political corruption are straightforward actions such as bribery (the giving of gifts to

*Visitors view gifts received by President and Mrs. George W. Bush on display at the White House Visitor Center. By law, all gifts to the president worth more than $200 are considered gifts to the office of the presidency.*

government officials in return for a government action), graft (the use of government expertise for self-enrichment), and extortion (the illegal use of one's official position or powers to obtain property, funds, or patronage). Other common forms of corruption include nepotism (favoring friends or relatives for government jobs), fraud (deception for personal gain), embezzlement (stealing government funds or property), and influence peddling (using influence with government officials to obtain favors for another person or group, usually for payment).

In the United States, all of these kinds of corruption are illegal, subject to various laws intended to root out corruption in government. For example, under U.S. laws, any gift to the president of the United States worth over two hundred dollars is considered a gift to the office of the presidency and not to the individual holding the office, and if an outgoing president wants to keep the gift, he or she must pay for it. Of course, even in the presence of laws, criminal penalties, and law enforcement, some individuals risk being caught. As the Randy "Duke" Cunningham case shows, the lure of easy money for some government officials is simply too enticing to turn down.

In some less developed or more autocratic countries, however, laws against corrupt behavior may be nonexistent, weak, or not enforced, and blatant corruption such as bribery, graft, and nepotism are built into the political system and present at the highest levels of government. In fact, many heads of state throughout world history have run organized systems of corruption in order to build their own wealth at the expense of the health and well-being of their people. Rulers such as Saddam Hussein in Iraq, Ferdinand Marcos in the Philippines, or Mohamed Suharto in Indonesia are prime examples of this type of top-level kleptomania.

Indeed, Suharto, who ruled Indonesia from 1976 to 1998, was named by the global anticorruption organization, Transparency

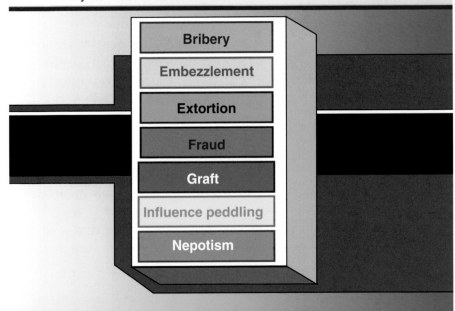

**Types of Corruption: A Sampling**

Many kinds of political corruption exist in government. All are illegal under U.S. law. However, in less developed countries or those with autocratic governments, if such laws exist, they may be weak or not enforced.

- Bribery
- Embezzlement
- Extortion
- Fraud
- Graft
- Influence peddling
- Nepotism

*Transparency International named former Indonesia president Mohamed Suharto the most corrupt world leader in the past twenty years.*

International (TI), as the most corrupt world leader of the past twenty years. He and his family reportedly stole between $15 billion and $35 billion from Indonesia's government during his thirty-plus-year rule. Under Suharto, the entire Indonesian economy was based on bribes to Suharto and his family. The system of corruption involved practices such as giving control of state-owned monopolies to family members and friends or requiring private companies to award stakes in the company to Suharto family members as a condition of navigating the government's bureaucratic process. In addition, under Suharto, all businesses and wealthy individuals were expected to send regular financial kickbacks, or "donations," to a variety of corrupt charitable foundations that functioned as Suharto's personal banks. Corruption in Indonesia during this period was truly systemic.

## Campaign Finance and Indirect Political Corruption

While outright bribery and nepotism may be the major concern in autocratic or developing countries, less direct forms of political corruption are more common in developed democracies. As Rose-Ackerman explains, "In democracies corruption scandals are frequently associated with the financing of political campaigns."[5] Because government officials in democracies must be elected to government positions in the executive and legislative branches, politicians become susceptible to allegations of campaign finance corruption when they accept large financial contributions from individuals, companies, unions, or interest groups to fund or support their campaigns. Although there is rarely any proof of vote buying or a similar, direct quid pro quo (something in return for something else) payment for campaign contributions, critics claim that politicians become beholden to their funding sources for reelection funds. Politicians are thus inclined to act in favor of this private interest rather than in the public interest when legislating or formulating government policies.

### POLITICAL FACTORS

"Money is a major factor in politics . . . but so are parties and constituents and issues and interest groups and regional alliances and ideological factions and gender and ethnicity, and a host of factors."

—Gerald C. Lubenow, director of the Citizen's Research Foundation, a campaign finance research institute at the University of California, Berkeley

Gerald C. Lubenow, ed., *The User's Guide to Campaign Finance Reform.* New York: Rowman & Littlefield, 2001, p. vii.

Campaign finance reform has been a major issue in American politics for many decades. In recent years it has only become more so as the costs of running a campaign for elected office have steadily spiraled to astronomical levels. Each election cycle, these campaign costs seem to rise, requiring prospective candidates and incumbents to amass huge amounts of money if they want to have any hope of successfully running for office or retaining their elected positions. Numerous reforms have been enacted, but new ways are found to circumvent each new legal requirement, allowing large amounts of private money to continue to pour into congressional and presidential elections. In fact, campaign finance is sometimes described by commentators as "legal corruption" because it often takes the form of large contributions that are technically legal under existing campaign finance laws.

## Links Between Lobbying, Corporate Fraud, and Corruption

Other forms of corruption that tend to arise in more developed, democratic countries concern the activities of high-paid lobbyists hired by corporations and interest groups to convince elected officials to support or oppose legislation or policies that might be either beneficial or harmful to their specific, private interests. Lobbyists also often help, behind the scenes, to coordinate and direct campaign contributions to elected officials. In fact, a lobbyist's job is to work tirelessly to keep the elected official informed of the interests of the lobbyist's employers, who are often major campaign funding sources.

Although the hiring and paying of professional lobbyists are usually not in themselves illegal, lobbyists in many countries are regulated to try to moderate their influence on government. In the United States, for example, the Lobbying Disclosure Act of 1995 requires lobbyists to register with the government and comply with certain disclosure requirements, and lobbyists are prohibited from bribing legislators with money or gifts. Today, there are close to thirty-five thousand lobbyists, most of them representing corporations or special-interest groups, who are registered to lobby the nation's 535 members of Congress and other government officials. Many of the lobbying firms maintain offices on K Street in Washington, D.C., an area known as the center for national-level lobbying activities.

In relatively rare cases, such as the Abramoff example, law enforcement is able to prove a case of direct bribery between lobbyists and government officials, where gifts, vacation trips, or financial rewards are unlawfully given by lobbyists to members of

*K Street in Washington, D.C., is the home of many lobbying firms.*

Congress to influence votes. For the most part, however, the influence of lobbyists and money is implied rather than explicit. The elected official simply knows implicitly that he or she is expected to favor the interests that funded his or her campaign. Although technically legal, many experts believe these implicit forces can be powerful influences on the way laws and policies are made and enforced by government.

Additional problems of corruption often arise with what is called the revolving door phenomenon. This is a common practice in the United States in which legislators, legislative staffers, or other government officials leave public office to take jobs as lobbyists for industry or special-interest groups, using their inside knowledge and contacts to influence legislation or government decisions to favor their new employers. According to Charles Lewis, the founder of the nonprofit research group Center for

Public Integrity, during the period between 1991 and 1996, 15 percent of former Senate aides and fourteen percent of former senior House of Representatives aides became registered lobbyists. As journalist Elizabeth Drew explains:

> The main sources of this pool of access-sharks were the "money committees," such as the House and Senate Commerce Committees, which handle such issues as banking and telecommunications. Sometimes the former aides so draw on their expertise and are so drawn into the legislative considerations that they in effect still act as staff members, writing legislation, except for a lot more money.[6]

Indeed, corporations and special-interest groups often pay their lobbyists a lot of money, and this financial temptation is difficult to turn down, especially after working for many years at relatively modest government-level salaries. Once again, the lure of money helps people ignore any moral or ethical misgivings and helps buy political influence for companies or groups that can afford it.

Critics also often draw connections between the role of money in political campaigns and corporate fraud that sometimes causes major financial losses for average citizens. Again, direct evidence of collusion between government officials and corporate leaders is uncommon, but in many cases pro-corporate government policies, or a lack of effective government oversight, are found to play a significant part in creating the conditions for corporate fraud. These conditions, critics claim, are the natural result of the close relationships between large industries and high-level politicians dependent on large campaign contributions. Reformers argue that large corporations have a type and level of political influence not available to most citizens and this influence sometimes results in corporate activities that bring great harm to taxpayers and the general public.

## The Threat to Democratic Principles

Many experts on political corruption argue as well that corruption within democratic governments undermines the values that form the central pillars of democracy. By producing legislators and officials who are accountable to corporate and special interests instead of citizens and taxpayers, these critics claim, corruption destroys the basic democratic principle that government must be representative of the people and work for the public good. Unaccountable or corrupt officials then, in turn, administer the government and make policies that often unfairly allocate government services and benefits. Meanwhile, corruption of the judiciary erodes another important pillar of democracy—the rule of law, the idea that objective rules govern all citizens and apply equally to all citizens to produce justice. A system that is corrupt and does not act in the public interest can ultimately become illegitimate in the eyes of its citizens, destroying the public's trust in their government.

In the United States, for example, some critics claim that corruption has become so widespread that it is changing the democratic system into one ruled by those with the most money. As Chicago political commentator Stephen Lendman puts it:

> The political game is rigged, the books are cooked and the notion that voters go to the polls to elect representatives who'll serve their interests is cockeyed hooey. The real game is "you scratch my back, and I'll scratch yours." But you better have lots of "scratch." . . . It's an incestuous relationship between powerful interests, usually big business and government with high-powered, well paid lobbyists "greasing the wheels" to make the system work. . . . The dirty game goes on and on and never ends.[7]

Reformers in the United States argue that fundamental reform of campaign financing, lobby restrictions, and similar remedies are necessary to protect the very essence of American democracy.

International aid organizations and donors such as the UN and the World Bank also see corruption as a threat to democracy in the developing world. They have begun programs to work with developing nations to help reduce corruption. By strengthening citizen participation in government, providing for freedom of speech and expression, and implementing reforms that require government leaders to report incomes, assets, campaign contributions, and other essential financial information, reformers believe they can help improve good governance and thereby reduce corruption around the globe.

## Effects of Corruption on Economic Development

Mounting evidence shows that, in addition to compromising democracy, corruption hinders economic development. When bribes are routine, the cost of doing business is increased and competition is reduced. Since only larger companies can afford to pay large bribes, corruption also disproportionately harms smaller businesses. These anticompetitive effects, in turn, often diminish the quality of products produced. Sometimes, widespread corruption in a country will even scare away potential foreign or domestic investors, drying up capital that might otherwise be available to help people start businesses or develop local

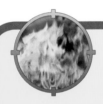

## Corruption and Health

A 2006 report on Global Health by Transparency International (TI) concludes that corruption has a dramatic effect on public health around the world. The report found that in both developed and less developed nations, significant amounts of public funds allocated for health projects are lost to fraud and corruption. In Cambodia, for example, TI found that between 5 percent and 10 percent of the health budget disappears before it is even transferred from the Ministry of Finance to the Ministry of Health. In places such as Russia, Asia, Africa, and South America, patients must bribe doctors and health care workers in order to get adequate health care. Even in the United States, the authors say, government-run health insurance programs such as Medicare and Medicaid lose 5–10 percent of their budget to overpayment of health claims. Also, the report argues that U.S. doctors are corrupted by drug companies that spend $2 billion each year on free meals and other gifts to advertise their drugs. TI claims that research shows doctors are influenced by their close relationships with drug manufacturers.

resources. Corruption, too, by influencing government officials to make bad decisions about how to spend government funds, draws public resources away from social expenditures such as education, health, and infrastructure (building and maintaining structures such as roads, bridges, airports, and utilities). This diversion of funds often contributes to increased poverty in highly corrupt countries.

## CORRUPTION NO LONGER INEVITABLE BY-PRODUCT

"Gone is the day when some pundits seriously argued that corruption was an efficient corrective for overregulated economies or that it should be tolerated as an inevitable by-product of intractable forces."

—Ben W. Heineman Jr. and Fritz Heimann

Ben W. Heineman Jr. and Fritz Heimann, "The Long War Against Corruption," *Foreign Affairs*, May/June 2006, p. 115.

Numerous studies have confirmed this negative link between corruption and economic development. As Harvard researcher Shang-Jin Wei concluded in a 1998 paper on the topic, "Evidence has clearly showed that domestic investment, foreign investment, and economic growth are lower in more corrupt countries."[8] Most experts today agree with Wei's conclusions. As Nancy Zucker Boswell and Peter Richardson of TI explained in 2003, "There is a global consensus that corruption in government and business inhibits economic growth and can perpetuate poverty."[9] Most experts also now reject a claim made by some in the past that bribes, by helping businesses to circumvent costly or burdensome regulations, can benefit a country's economy.

## Typical Reform Proposals

A variety of techniques have been used to combat political corruption, but determining the appropriate remedies often depends on the diverse conditions of corruption that exist in each country. Nevertheless, experts tend to agree on several elements that appear conducive to positive reform. For less developed nations, experts say it is critical to create government transparency—a system for freedom of information, mandatory government reporting, open meeting and other citizen participation laws designed to provide information to the public about the actions and decisions of government. It is also important for nations to enact laws geared to preventing corruption, such as antibribery and conflict-of-interest laws, codes of ethics, and whistle-blower provisions that encourage government employees to report corrupt conduct. In addition, to reduce the lure of bribes, civil service reforms are often necessary to ensure that government employees are reasonably paid and chosen based on merit rather than through patronage or nepotism (family connections). None of these measures can be effective, however, without competent criminal prosecutors and an independent judiciary to enforce anticorruption laws.

For more developed countries such as the United States, which already have these types of basic anticorruption and transparency laws and which face problems involving the increasing role of money in elections and lobbying, the prescription is different. Here, reformers suggest a variety of solutions such as campaign finance restrictions; strategies for countering the influence of money in elections (such as offering public financing and free TV airtime to candidates); and efforts to combat the revolving door syndrome, such as restrictions on where government employees can work once they leave government service.

Not everyone agrees that corruption is always corrosive or that reform is necessary, however. Some analysts in the United States, for example, argue that the right to spend money on politics is a form of free speech protected by the Constitution and that there is no concrete proof that money buys influence. They reason that the need for money focuses candidates on issues that matter most to those willing to give money and not just their vote. These views have sometimes been effective in court, but they are increasingly at odds with both expert and public opinion. For most people, political corruption is an inherent evil that must be fought.

# CHAPTER 2

# POLITICAL CORRUPTION IN AMERICA

Money and corruption have been features of American democracy since its inception. Historically, U.S. political elections have been privately financed, and early in the nation's history, it was routine for wealthy speculators and entrepreneurs to pour large amounts of money into politics to buy votes, influence, and favors. As the country matured, however, anticorruption laws were passed to try to limit corrupt political influences. A series of important reforms were passed in the early part of the twentieth century, and major campaign finance reforms followed in the wake of one of America's most notorious political scandals—Watergate. The floodgates to corruption, however, reopened in 1974, when a U.S. Supreme Court decision undercut many of these reforms and once again allowed huge amounts of money to flow into the U.S. political system.

## A Tradition of Corruption

During America's early years, the notion of public service was quite different from today: Bribes, favoritism, and other forms of what we now call corruption were commonplace and accepted. Colonial governors sent from England supplemented their salaries by amassing large land holdings and other wealth through illegal dealings, and merchants made huge profits off the Revolutionary War by charging exorbitant prices for goods needed by soldiers. Indeed, the country was literally built on a tradition of corruption. Later, as the country industrialized and spread westward, powerful businessmen and ruthless speculators routinely used bribes to buy political influence and manipulate government policies in ways that yielded great fortunes for themselves and their associates. In fact, even President Abraham Lincoln tolerated widespread graft from his first war secretary, Simon Cameron, who presided over countless numbers of transportation and munitions contracts designed largely to plunder the national treasury during the Civil War.

One of the most corrupt presidential administrations in America's early history, however, was that of Ulysses S. Grant. The Union's top general during the Civil War, Grant became a national hero and was elected president at war's end. As the country

*Corruption was common during America's early years. Simon Cameron, President Lincoln's first war secretary, was involved in corruption during the Civil War.*

turned from war to peace, the same group of crooked businessmen who amassed fortunes profiteering from the war effort began
to do business with the federal government, turning it into a massive spoils system to benefit a greedy few. One of the most famous
scandals during Grant's term, however, was the Black Friday gold
conspiracy, a scheme launched by war profiteers Jim Fisk and Jay
Gould. The two tried to corner the nation's gold market by buying up gold and inflating the price so they could sell at an enormous profit. The conspiracy brought financial ruin to many Wall
Street investors in 1869.

High levels of corruption also haunted state and local politics
during this period. As the political magazine the *Nation* complained in 1868, "There is hardly a legislature in the country that
is not suspected of corruption; there is hardly a court over which
the same suspicion does not hang."[10] In fact, this was the era of
the notorious William M. "Boss" Tweed, a New York politician
who was elected to the House of Representatives in 1852, the
New York City Board of Advisors in 1856, and the New York State

*William M. "Boss" Tweed ran the New York political machine Tammany Hall.*

POLITICAL MARKET.

*This mid-nineteenth-century cartoon shows how easily government officials could be bribed by ruthless businessmen.*

Senate in 1867. Tweed also ran Tammany Hall, a Democratic party political machine that was at the heart of New York political thievery for many decades. Tweed helped to get politicians elected by organizing the city's many new immigrants and buying votes. Politicians then looked the other way while Tweed and his cronies skimmed as much as $200 million from the New York City government. Tweed was convicted of forgery and larceny in 1873, but his system of political patronage and corruption remained a powerful force in New York City politics for many more years. By the time America celebrated its one hundredth birthday in 1876, both the national and local governments were still permeated with bribery, graft, and political patronage.

## The Progressive Push for Anticorruption Laws

The public's disgust with America's long history of corruption eventually produced a number of reforms. As early as the 1880s, industrialization and the massive wave of corruption that followed the Civil War created a push for social reforms across society led by people who called themselves Progressives. Progressives soon convinced Congress to pass the first political reform—the Pendleton Act of 1883—legislation that created the nation's first merit-based civil service system. Prior to this time, government jobs were obtained only through a system of patronage, in which jobs were given to friends, relatives, or those who offered bribes. In the 1880s, for example, it was not uncommon for newspapers to carry ads such as the following: "WANTED— A GOVERNMENT CLERKSHIP at a salary of not less than $1,000 per annum. Will give $100 to any one securing me such a position."[11] The Pendleton Act established a system of civil service exams, which allowed federal government jobs for the first time to be filled based on qualifications. It also prohibited federal workers from making contributions to political campaigns in order to get or keep their jobs.

By cutting off the stream of payments from federal workers and job seekers, however, the Pendleton Act helped to increase corporate contributions to political campaigns, a phenomenon that had been growing since at least the end of the Civil War. In the 1896 presidential race, for example, wealthy Cleveland industrialist Marcus Alonzo Hanna raised a staggering $4 million ($82 million in today's dollars) for Republican candidate William McKinley. McKinley spent more than ten times the amount spent by his opponent, Democrat William Jennings Bryan, and this fat bankroll is credited with propelling McKinley into the White House. By the end of the nineteenth century, the amount of corporate money in elections had reached alarming levels.

The 1904 presidential election, however, marked a turning point for American campaign financing. When Democratic challenger Alton B. Parker accused Theodore Roosevelt of accepting large corporate contributions during his campaign, Roosevelt responded by proposing a ban on all corporate contributions.

Roosevelt's call for reform was taken up by Progressive activists and finally answered by Congress in 1907 with the passage of the Tillman Act, a law that prohibited corporations and national banks from contributing to federal campaigns. The Tillman Act was truly landmark legislation—the first federal law to address campaign financing.

Thereafter, Progressives continued to press for more reforms, arguing that publicizing the source of campaign donations would allow citizens to evaluate whether legislators were beholden to contributors. This pressure resulted in the 1910 Publicity Act, which as amended in 1911 required federal congressional candidates to disclose fully all spending and contributions at the end of election campaigns. The act also established the first spending limits for federal campaigns: five thousand dollars for House campaigns and ten thousand dollars for Senate contests. The spending limits, however, were quickly challenged, and in 1921, the Supreme Court in *Newberry v. United States* struck down the

*William McKinley spent ten times more than his opponent on advertising.*

spending limits, ruling that Congress had no authority to regulate primary elections.

## Teapot Dome and More Reforms

Despite these reforms, a scandal in the 1920s showed that high-level corruption continued to be a problem in the federal government. The election of President Warren G. Harding in 1920 led to Teapot Dome, a political scandal involving the leasing of oil fields located on public lands. Harding's friend and secretary of the interior, Albert B. Fall, awarded a series of long-term lease contracts worth about $200 million to two large U.S. oil companies in exchange for loans and gifts totaling more than four hundred thousand dollars. When Fall's sudden prosperity attracted attention, Harding steadfastly defended him, but Fall was eventually convicted of bribery in 1929 and sentenced to one year in prison. Fall, however, was only one of many corrupt Harding appointees. As author Nathan Miller explains:

> [Harding's] interior secretary became the first cabinet member to go to jail; his attorney general only narrowly escaped a similar fate; and his secretary of the navy was forced to resign as a result of a mixture of stupidity and criminal negligence. Fraud in the Veterans Bureau, graft in the Office of the Alien Property Custodian, and conspiracy in the Justice Department were all part of Harding's legacy.[12]

The corruption in Harding's administration helped rally support for more reform efforts and led to the passage of yet another piece of reform legislation—the Federal Corrupt Practices Act of 1925. Although it exempted primary elections because of the *Newberry* decision, this legislation once again established campaign spending limits for candidates running in congressional races (Senate campaigns—twenty-five thousand dollars; House campaigns—five thousand dollars) and required national political parties to file reports of their contributions and expenditures. In addition, the law tightened previous disclosure rules by requiring quarterly reports, even in nonelection years.

Two other reforms were enacted during this era. One was the Hatch Act of 1939, amended in 1940. This law supplemented the

*An artist's representation of the Teapot Dome Scandal.*

provisions of the Pendleton Act by prohibiting various forms of political activity by federal workers. Among the banned activities was the practice of having federal employees solicit campaign contributions, then a common source of revenue for state and local political parties. The law also set limits for federal campaign contributions—a limit of five thousand dollars per year for individual contributions and a limit of $3 million on the total amount that could be collected by political parties. The final reform during this time was the War Labor Disputes Act of 1943, which included a provision prohibiting labor unions from making political contributions to federal candidates.

## CULTURE OF MONEY

"The culture of money dominates Washington as never before; money now rivals or even exceeds power as the preeminent goal."
—Elizabeth Drew, journalist and author of numerous books about the U.S. government and politics

Elizabeth Drew, *The Corruption of American Politics: What Went Wrong and Why.* New York: Overlook, 1999, p. 64.

## Business as Usual

Although well-intended, many of the early anticorruption reforms failed to accomplish their stated aims. The cornerstone Tillman Act, for example, was quickly circumvented by corporations; businesses simply awarded bonuses to their employees with the understanding that the employees would give the money to candidates endorsed by the company. Other laws, such as the Publicity Act, failed to include enforcement mechanisms. Spending limits, too, were largely ignored. As political scientist Frank Sorauf has put it, "The reality was one of pervasive evasion and nonenforcement."[13]

As a result, large amounts of corporate money continued to pour into politics in the 1950s, 1960s, and 1970s. New technologies, such as radio and television, were added to the existing publicity tools of newspaper ads and billboards, and election campaigns became increasingly more expensive. Television, in particular, revolutionized politics and dramatically affected the costs of political campaigns. As Sorauf has noted, "Television costs in the general election of 1956 had been $6.6 million, but by 1968 they had shot up to $27.1 million."[14]

This period, however, did not produce the types of large-scale bribery scandals seen in the past. Nathan Miller explains:

The Harding scandals were the last hurrah of old-fashioned thievery on the national level. In the wake of the New

Deal [Franklin D. Roosevelt's political program], World War II, and the Cold War [the standoff between the United States and Russia following World War II], big-time corruption became the domain of big business and industry. . . . Corruption became more sophisticated, more subtle.[15]

Nevertheless, corruption scandals did not go away. During Harry S. Truman's administration (1945–1953), several officials appointed by the president became involved in small-time bribery incidents, bringing great embarrassment to Truman. One of these officials was General Harry Vaughan, who used his influence with the White House to help certain companies gain preferential treatment from government agencies. In return, Vaughan was given several deep freezers, a scarce commodity in the postwar period. The freezers became a symbol of corruption for the Truman administration.

The Truman scandals helped elect war hero Dwight D. Eisenhower to the presidency in 1952, but revelations about annual payments by millionaires to Eisenhower's running mate, Senator Richard M. Nixon, almost doomed the Eisenhower campaign.

*Richard Nixon giving his famous "Checkers" speech.*

Nixon managed to survive by making an emotional speech on nationwide television—a speech referred to as "Checkers" because he claimed the only gift he had ever accepted was a cocker spaniel dog named Checkers. Nevertheless, the Eisenhower administration, as well as the subsequent administrations of John F. Kennedy and Lyndon B. Johnson, each included disclosures of bribery and corruption. Presidential candidates also spent progressively more money in each election.

## MORE REPETITION OF POSITIVE ADS

"People don't like . . . [negative ads], but they work. . . . Repetition is what it takes to make the message stick, and positive ads need a lot more repetition than negative ones."
—Steve McMahon, founder of McMahon, Squier and Associates, a media consulting firm in the Washington, D.C., area

Quoted in Mark Green, *Selling Out: How Big Corporate Money Buys Elections, Rams Through Legislation, and Betrays Our Democracy.* New York: Regan, 2002, p. 116. www.thirdworldtraveler.com/Election_Reform/Campaigning_Money_SO.html.

By the 1970s, concerns over campaign costs once again created a climate for reform. In 1971, Congress responded to these concerns with two major reform bills. The Revenue Act authorized a public financing plan that allowed taxpayers to indicate on their federal tax returns that they wanted to donate one dollar of their taxes to a public campaign fund for presidential and vice presidential campaigns. The second piece of legislation was the 1971 Federal Election Campaign Act (FECA), a law that replaced earlier reporting and disclosure requirements with a strengthened plan that required candidates and parties to disclose more detailed information. FECA also applied to political parties and political action committees (PACs), groups formed to raise money for political candidates. In addition, in an effort to limit rising campaign costs, the act limited the amount federal candidates—both congressional and presidential—could contribute to their own campaigns as well as the amounts that could be spent on all media advertising, including television, radio, magazines, newspapers, and billboards.

# Iran-Contra

The most well-known political scandal of the Reagan years was Iran-Contra, a 1986 scandal involving the sale of military arms to Iran, a U.S. enemy, in order to free American hostages held by the terrorist group Hizballah. The profits from these arms sales were then used secretly to fund an anti-Communist insurgent group, the Contras, that was fighting to overturn the Nicaraguan government. The operation was run by William Casey, Reagan's director of the Central Intelligence Agency, and Marine Lieutenant Colonel Oliver L. North, a staffer at the National Security Council. The selling of arms to Iran in exchange for hostages violated Reagan's stated policy of never bargaining with terrorists for hostages, and the provision of aid to the Contras was a direct violation of a law (the Boland Amendment) prohibiting such activities. Just as in Watergate, high-level government officials broke the law to achieve political power and policy goals.

An investigation produced several criminal convictions, but Casey died before the investigation was completed, and North's conviction for perjury was overturned on technicalities. Six other Iran-Contra defendants, including secretary of defense Caspar Weinberger, were pardoned by Reagan vice president George H.W. Bush after he was elected president.

*Oliver North testifies during the Iran-Contra hearings.*

## Watergate Reforms

An array of much more serious reforms, however, followed in the wake of Watergate, one of the biggest political scandals ever to hit the United States. The scandal began in 1972 when operatives of then president Richard Nixon, a Republican, burglarized and bugged the offices of the Democratic National Committee in the Watergate building in Washington, D.C., in order to obtain political advantage. A subsequent investigation revealed that Nixon's reelection committee had also created a secret and illegal campaign fund containing hundreds of thousands of dollars of undisclosed corporate donations—funds that were tapped to buy the silence of the Watergate burglars during their criminal trials. Later investigations revealed that Nixon also relied on huge corporate contributions for his presidential campaigns and that large amounts had been given by people who were rewarded with ambassadorships from the Nixon administration. Nixon was forced to resign in 1974, and over the next several years, Congress devoted itself to passing a series of laws known as the Watergate reforms.

The most significant reform of this period was a 1974 amendment to FECA that virtually rewrote the original law. The most important part of the new law was the creation of the first program of public campaign funding for presidential elections. This program allowed U.S. presidential candidates to opt for full public financing for general election campaigns and partial subsidies for primary campaigns in exchange for limiting private donations. Its purpose was to reduce the pressures of raising money for campaigns and encourage candidates to solicit small donations. The program operated through a voluntary contribution on federal income tax forms, the same idea contained in the Revenue Act of 1971 (which had not yet been implemented).

## REPRESENTING SMALLER CAUSES

"It is difficult to represent the little fellow when the big fellow pays the tab."
—Robert Reich, secretary of labor during the Bill Clinton presidency, currently a professor of law at Northeastern University

Quoted in Mark Green, *Selling Out: How Big Corporate Money Buys Elections, Rams Through Legislation, and Betrays Our Democracy.* New York: Regan, 2002, p. 116. www.thirdworldtraveler.com/Election_Reform/Campaigning_Money_ SO.html.

The act also strengthened disclosure provisions and set new limits on campaign contributions and expenditures. Individual contribution limits were set at one thousand dollars per candidate, an additional one thousand dollars for candidate advertising, five thousand dollars for donations to PACs, and an aggregate amount of twenty-five thousand dollars for all contributions to all

*The Watergate complex in Washington, D.C. Thirty years ago, burglars working for President Nixon broke into the Democratic National Committee offices here, leading to one of the biggest political scandals in U.S. history.*

federal candidates, parties, or PACs. PACs were permitted to collect only small donations of five thousand dollars each year from individuals and were limited to contributing five thousand dollars per candidate. Candidates themselves were limited to spending only fifty thousand dollars of their own money if they wanted to accept public financing. To enforce these provisions, the act created an independent agency—the Federal Election Commission.

Watergate also produced a series of other government reforms. The 1974 Freedom of Information Act, for example, was enacted to allow ordinary citizens to hold government accountable by obtaining copies of public documents and records. The 1976 Government in Sunshine Act required federal government agencies to conduct open meetings with certain exceptions. In 1978 Congress passed the Ethics in Government Act, which created a special prosecutor (later called independent counsel) position that could be used by Congress or the attorney general to investigate the conduct of persons holding high office. Also in 1978, Congress enacted federal whistle-blower legislation to prevent retaliation against persons who expose government corruption.

### *Buckley v. Valeo*

FECA and the other Watergate reforms were a major step forward in the battle against corruption. However, in 1976, the U.S. Supreme Court dealt a death blow to many of FECA's provisions. In a landmark case called *Buckley v. Valeo*, the Court ruled parts of the act unconstitutional because they violated the First Amendment. For the first time, the court ruled the act of spending money for political campaigns was entitled to constitutional free speech protections. Specifically, the ruling eliminated all FECA's spending limits as well as limits on contributions made by candidates themselves or made by citizens or PACs for so-called independent expenditures, such as advertising that was not connected with a candidate's campaign. The Court upheld the remaining parts of FECA—its disclosure requirements, the public financing program, and the individual, party, and PAC limits on direct campaign contributions.

# Criticism of *Buckley v. Valeo*

Since it was issued in 1976, the U.S. Supreme Court's decision in *Buckley v. Valeo* has aroused frequent criticism. Many experts on campaign finance reform believe that *Buckley's* ruling—that limits on campaign spending were an unconstitutional infringement on the free speech rights of candidates—was badly reasoned. Constitutional law holds that limits on free speech are permissible only if they serve a compelling government interest. The *Buckley* Court found that the only compelling governmental interest would be prevention of corruption, and that spending limits failed to serve this interest. Critics charge, however, that there are other extremely compelling interests at stake, such as the need to maintain a fully representative democracy, in which elected officials represent public rather than private interests. The Court's failure to consider this larger issue, critics say, is the primary reason that the United States has been unable to control the problem of money in politics. Despite this criticism, the Court has shown no signs that it intends to overturn or modify the *Buckley* ruling. As recently as June 2006, in *Randall v. Sorrell*, the Court upheld *Buckley* in striking down a Vermont law limiting political spending.

The *Buckley* decision is credited by most experts for unleashing a new wave of corporate money into elections. The decision allowed unlimited amounts to be spent on campaigns and resulted in more wealthy candidates running for office. Also, by introducing the concept of independent expenditures, *Buckley* encouraged a whole new trend of "issue ads"—expensive television advertisements usually funded by PACs set up by corporations and other special-interest groups. As long as the ads were independent, meaning that they did not coordinate directly with campaigns or use any of a list of words that the Court said would constitute express advocacy on behalf of or against a candidate (such as *vote for*, *elect*, or *defeat*), there was absolutely no limit to the amount of money that could be spent.

Not surprisingly, after *Buckley*, the number of PACs skyrocketed, and issue ads, often negative ones, became the new weapon of choice in political campaigns. One of the earliest and most memorable negative issue ads was one that aired in the 1988 election between then vice president George H.W. Bush and Democratic challenger Michael Dukakis. Bush faced an uphill battle against Dukakis, who as governor of Massachusetts had compiled an excellent record of reviving the state economy. Bush won the election, however, thanks largely to a classic negative ad run by the conservative National Security Political Action Committee featuring a black felon named Willie Horton, a convicted murderer. The ads charged that Dukakis was soft on crime since Horton was awarded a weekend pass from a Massachusetts prison—a weekend that he used to kidnap a couple, stab the man, and rape the woman.

Bush supporters used negative ads again in the 1992 election between then president George H.W. Bush and Democratic challenger Bill Clinton. In that race, a conservative lobbying group called the Christian Action Network used a negative television commercial to criticize Clinton's support for homosexual rights. The $2 million ad aired over 250 times in twenty-four major cities across the country and featured Clinton policy statements interspersed with pictures of young men wearing chains and leather marching in a Gay Pride parade. At the end, the ad asked, "Is this your vision for a better America?" The Federal Election

Commission challenged the ad, arguing that its use of negative imagery constituted express advocacy under *Buckley*. The commission, however, lost in federal court because the words explicitly banned by *Buckley* were not used. Since then, the use of issue ads has exploded.

## Bundling and Soft Money Loopholes

Additional loopholes were also found to circumvent FECA. Using one technique called bundling, for example, individuals or companies can collect large numbers of individual contributions from family members, friends, or employees and then deliver the combined donation to a particular candidate with a clear understanding of who is responsible for collecting the money. This makes candidates as beholden as if that person or company had directly made the large donation.

### POLITICS AND MONEY

"Money cannot be entirely eliminated from politics. Elections must be financed and wealthy interests concerned with legislative outcomes and government policy may be willing to foot the bill."
— Susan Rose-Ackerman, professor of law and political science at Yale University and codirector of the Yale Law School's Center for Law, Economics, and Public Policy

Susan Rose-Ackerman, *Government and Corruption: Causes, Consequences, and Reform.* New York: Cambridge University Press, 1999, pp. 132–33.

Soft money, which refers to funds not regulated by federal laws, is a bit more complicated. Because state and local political parties complained that the FECA spending limits restricted them from doing grassroots political activities such as voter registration and get-out-the-vote drives, Congress passed new amendments to FECA in 1979 granting party organizations a limited exemption from spending limits. Under the new law, as interpreted by the Federal Election Commission, parties could collect and spend unlimited amounts of money on these types of local political activities. Soon, however, political parties began funding issue ads as well, stretching the limits of FECA to new levels. This dramatically expanded the role of political parties in campaigns, allowing them to become the primary sponsor of expensive issue ads.

Eventually, all of these loopholes completely gutted the anti-corruption reforms put in place after Watergate. Although donations to candidates were still subject to limits, unlimited amounts of soft money could now be contributed to buy ads and otherwise indirectly support specific candidates. As journalist Elizabeth Drew explains: "As of the 1996 election, the post-Watergate reforms . . . had been rendered null and void. . . . The idea that there were any limits on raising and spending private money for presidential candidates who accepted public financing was rendered obsolete."[16]

# CHAPTER 3

# MONEY AND POLITICAL CORRUPTION IN THE UNITED STATES

Today, thanks to the weaknesses in U.S. election laws, millionaires, corporations, unions, and special-interest groups continue to pour vast amounts of money into elections and lobbying. Although candidates benefit by receiving large amounts of campaign funds, they no longer have control over their own campaigns and have to spend much of their time focused on raising those funds. In addition, critics claim that money has created a deeply entrenched culture of corruption in Washington that is responsible for numerous recent political and corporate scandals and that is at the root of government decisions that have proved disastrous for ordinary Americans.

## The Effect on Candidates and Incumbents

The biggest effect of *Buckley v. Valeo* and the loopholes in campaign finance laws is an enormous increase in the amount of money it takes to win elections. As Democratic politician and author Mark Green explains, "While in 1976 it cost an average of $87,000 to win a House seat and $609,000 a U.S. Senate seat, those amounts grew by 2000 like beanstalks to $842,000 for the House and $7.2 million for the Senate—a tenfold leap."[17] Today, experts say it is no longer possible to run for the Senate in any state in the nation with less than $3 million in campaign funds, and some Senate campaigns have cost much more. Hillary Clinton, for example, spent $30 million to acquire her Senate seat, and even that was far less than the record of $63 million spent by Jon Corzine in his 2000 New Jersey campaign.

Presidential elections, too, cost more each year. In the 2004 presidential election, for example, President George W. Bush and Senator John Kerry both rejected public funding during the primary phase, allowing them together to raise almost a billion dollars in private financing; then, during the general election, they each received an additional $74.6 million in government funding. These figures made the 2004 presidential election the most expensive in American history.

The major cost in campaigns is the increasingly expensive broadcast time for TV ads. Free airtime is not mandated, and even scheduled debates between the candidates are sometimes not broadcast by the various television networks. The candidate who does not win the fund-raising battle usually loses the election. In fact, the overwhelming majority (94 percent) of congressional races are won by the big spenders, regardless of the candidates' qualifications, skills, or voting records.

Experts say the quest for big money has changed the way the president and members of Congress run for office. Today, fund-raising is the paramount priority during campaigns. As Mark Green explains: "Thanks to today's high-cost races, candidates spend very little time running in the traditional sense of the word—mobilizing voters, communicating ideas, debating opponents, attending public meetings. Instead, candidates fund-raise for office. Their time is dominated by the incessant chore of pleading, cajoling, schmoozing for campaign cash."[18]

The emphasis on fund-raising continues once candidates are elected. In fact, Green claims that "senators from the ten largest states have to raise an average of over $34,000 a week, every week, for six years to stay in office."[19] Critics claim this preoccupation with raising money negatively affects politicians' job performance. Both congressional representatives and presidents,

*Jon Corzine spent a record $63 million during his 2000 campaign for New Jersey's Senate seat.*

for example, are spending fewer and fewer days on the people's business. For many legislators, Fridays, weekends, and Mondays are devoted to fund-raising efforts, leaving only three days for legislative work. Often too, critics say there is a widespread reluctance by incumbents to take on controversial issues or issues unpopular with major funding sources, for fear of losing the career-sustaining campaign dollars. In light of legislators' pressing money priorities, some commentators say it is no wonder that Congress has developed a reputation among voters for doing nothing.

## MONEY CAN AFFECT YOUR VIEWPOINT

"If the only people you ever talk to are people with the wherewithal to contribute thousands of dollars to your campaign, that is bound to affect the way you see the world."

—James Carville, the strategist for Bill Clinton's successful presidential campaign in 1992, today a well-known political consultant, commentator, and pundit who, together with fellow commentator Paul Begala, serves as a regular contributor on CNN's program *The Situation Room*

James Carville and Paul Begala, "Not One Dime: A Radical Plan to Abramoff-Proof Politics," *Washington Monthly*, March 2006, p. 14.

If incumbents ever forget who is paying for their reelection, the army of corporate and special-interest lobbyists will quickly remind them. As the representatives for their employers, these lobbyists facilitate all kinds of contributions that bring money or other benefits to members of Congress or their districts. These include not only direct campaign contributions from company employees and PACs but also unlimited soft money donations for fund-raising dinners and events, charitable organizations favored by legislators, or special projects that might bring jobs or tourist dollars to a legislator's home state or district. The same system infects the executive branch.

All this money buys enormous access to Congress as well as to other government and administration officials—close contact that ordinary citizens do not have. Although sometimes this access may buy officials' votes or decisions on key policies or pieces of legislation, usually the result is much more subtle but equally important forms of influence. In Congress this might include voting to prevent bills or certain bill provisions from ever being reported out of congressional committees, the quiet insertion of obscure provisions benefiting a private interest into larger bills that are sure to pass, or the addition of spending earmarks to provide federal funding for pet projects. Access might also convince government officials to block or change government regulations, influence regulatory decisions, help secure government contract awards, or achieve some other form of behind-the-scenes advocacy that benefits campaign donors. Reformers say big money in politics unquestionably results in government policies that are geared toward the needs of corporate contributors rather than the needs of ordinary citizens. These effects are often very difficult to prove, and most of the time they are hidden from the general public. Sometimes, however, information about this system leaks out, resulting in much-publicized scandals and causing the public to suspect all politicians of corruption. As Republican senator John McCain said: "We're all tainted. . . . [All members of Congress are] under suspicion as long as Washington is awash in special-interest money."[20]

## Modern Political Corruption Scandals

Since the last set of reforms in the 1970s, America has experienced a host of modern corruption scandals affecting virtually every recent presidential administration. Even reform-minded Jimmy Carter, the first president after Watergate, suffered from minor scandals during his 1977–1981 term in office. His own brother, Billy Carter, for example, accepted a $220,000 loan from Libya to facilitate oil sales to America, and the press accused him of selling his influence with the White House.

The administration of President Ronald Reagan in the 1980s, however, brought some of the most serious political scandals in the nation's history. As Nathan Miller explains:

> While preaching against waste, fraud, and abuse of government power, he [Reagan] presided for eight years over an administration that combined the old-fashioned graft of the Grant and Harding eras with an undisguised

grab for power. . . . Thievery and manipulation occurred on a grand scale and the amount of loot took a quantum leap compared to previous corruption.[21]

Among the scandals that arose during Reagan's term of office was a major corruption investigation of the Department of Housing and Urban Development (HUD) and its secretary, Samuel R. Pierce Jr. Although HUD was supposed to help with housing for the poor, under Pierce's reign, HUD funds were used to build luxury country clubs, golf courses, and other projects favored by members of Congress or government officials. HUD officials were also found to have embezzled funds and directed projects without competitive bidding to Reagan supporters. In fact, secretary of the interior James Watt was indicted for using connections at HUD to secure federal funds for housing projects developed by his private clients. Neither Pierce nor Reagan took steps to halt the widespread corruption at HUD.

## THE HOLD OF WEALTH ON POLITICS

"Money is choking our democracy to death. Our elections are bought out from under us and our public officials are doing the bidding of mercenaries. So powerful is the hold of wealth on politics that we cannot say America is working for all Americans. The majority may support such broad social goals as affordable medical coverage for all, decent wages for working people, safe working conditions, a secure retirement, and clean air and water, but there is no government 'of, by, and for the people' to deliver on those aspirations."

—Bill Moyers, a veteran television journalist who is currently president of the Schumann Center for Media and Democracy, a foundation dedicated to renewing the democratic process

Bill Moyers, "A Culture of Corruption," *Washington Spectator,* April 1, 2006. www.truth out.org/docs_2006/040806G.shtml.

Reagan's laissez-faire attitude toward corruption contributed to numerous instances of corruption in other parts of the government as well. A scandal surrounding a defense contractor called Wedtech, for example, resulted in the conviction of Reagan's press secretary

Lyn Nofziger for lobbying the White House on behalf of Wedtech too soon after leaving government (although his conviction was later overturned) and in the resignation of attorney general Edwin Meese, who had worked as a lobbyist for Wedtech before his appointment to the Justice Department. Indeed, by the end of Reagan's presidency, as Miller explains, "as many as 225 of his appointees faced allegations of ethical or criminal wrongdoing."[22]

Subsequent presidential administrations have also been criticized for activities that, at the very least, give the appearance of corruption. George H.W. Bush, for example, was frequently linked with international influence-peddling deals during his 1989–1993 presidential term. According to political analyst Kevin Phillips, a number of Bush's relatives made personal fortunes during his presidency. Bush's brothers, for example, both made large amounts of money arranging U.S. deals for Asian companies, while Bush's sons Jeb, Marvin, and Lee Bush acquired high-paying jobs and made numerous real estate investments and other deals largely with the help of President Bush's network of wealthy fund-raisers and supporters. These scenarios suggested that Bush's relatives may have been selling their influence with the administration to acquire personal gain.

Meanwhile, Bush's son George W. Bush (who was later elected president) acquired shares in Harken Energy, a small company with no overseas oil-drilling experience that nevertheless, during his father's presidency, won a major oil-drilling contract from Bahrain as well as direct access to President Bush and his foreign policy advisers. In 1990, son George W. made a quick $848,000 profit by abruptly selling his Harken shares just before Harken stock prices dropped dramatically because of the Gulf War and deteriorating finances. The Securities and

*Under secretary Samuel R. Pierce Jr., there was widespread corruption at the Department of Housing and Urban Development (HUD).*

*The Wedtech scandal led to the resignation of attorney general Edwin Meese during the Reagan years.*

Exchange Commission, then headed by former aide to President Bush, Richard Breeden, investigated the deal for illegal insider trading but issued no ruling against the president's son. The most valuable benefit to George W., however, came when he was given the opportunity to buy a stake in the valuable Texas Rangers baseball team, owned by two major political contributors to his father, for a mere $600,000 of borrowed money. In 1998, Bush sold his Rangers shares for $15 million, making him a rich man and positioning him for a political career.

Several George H.W. Bush administration officials, too, were criticized for conflicts-of-interest that brought them personal riches. One was treasury secretary James A. Baker, who approved policies that benefited U.S. banks while he held a large chunk of stock in one bank, Chemical Bank, resulting in a 40 percent personal profit. Also, Bush campaign manager James A. Lake reportedly was paid two hundred thousand dollars every three months to represent the interests of Sheik Zayed ibn Sultan al Nuhayan of Abu Dhabi with the U.S. government.

Nor did the next U.S. president, Bill Clinton, escape corruption criticisms. Some of the most serious allegations against Clinton occurred when news leaked out that the People's Republic of China tried to make numerous large donations to the Democratic National Committee (DNC) and other democratic causes just before the 1996 presidential election. Such donations by foreign citizens or governments to U.S. political candidates or campaigns are illegal under U.S. law. The largest donations, including a $460,000 cash donation to Clinton's legal defense fund and $220,000 to the DNC, were made by Yah Lin "Charlie" Trie, a Chinese American friend of Clinton's suspected of working for the Chinese. Clinton and other officials also met frequently with a number of other Chinese Americans who had close ties to China and contributed large amounts to the DNC, suggesting that they too may have been agents of the People's Republic of China. Also, attorney general Janet Reno refused calls for the appointment of an independent counsel to look into the possibility of widespread fund-raising abuses by the administration, sparking rumors of a cover-up. The Justice Department's own investigation, however, yielded seventeen convictions for campaign finance irregularities, many of them against Clinton friends such as Trie.

The nation's next president, George W. Bush, has been repeatedly criticized for his questionable business dealings and easy acquisition of wealth during his father's presidential term as well as for corruption within his own administration. David Safavian, Bush's administrator for the Office of Management and Budget, the chief purchasing agency for the federal government, for example, became the first person arrested in the 2006 Jack Abramoff lobbying scandal. Safavian, a good friend of Abramoff, was found guilty by a jury in June 2006 on five felony counts for obstruction and lying during a government investigation into the lobbying scandal.

Another scandal during the George W. Bush administration involved the award of multibillion-dollar Iraq war contracts to Halliburton, a company once headed by vice president Dick Cheney, and other companies with close ties to the administration, without engaging in a competitive bidding process. As the war progressed, government investigators discovered that a Halliburton subsidiary had grossly overcharged the U.S. government for supplies

*Former U.S. president Bill Clinton has been criticized for corruption scandals.*

*Halliburton has been accused of war profiteering. This sign was posted by protesters at an annual Halliburton shareholders meeting.*

such as meals and fuel—an example of war profiteering similar to past war scandals.

## Congressional Corruption Scandals

Like the executive branch, the legislative branch has endured its own share of corruption scandals during recent years. In the late 1980s, the scandal surrounding defense contractor Wedtech became the focus of an investigation that found that Wedtech had hired numerous lobbyists, including some members of Congress, to help land lucrative federal contracts. The lobbying was not reported and included outright bribing of government officials. Eventually, about twenty state, local, and federal government officials were convicted on charges of bribery and related crimes. Among those convicted were members of Congress, such as New

York Democratic congressman Mario Biaggi. In 1989, both House Speaker Jim Wright and majority whip Tony Coelho were forced to resign due to numerous charges of ethics irregularities and petty corruption involving activities such as receiving special deals on stock trades, profiting from inflated book sales to interest groups, and having relatives work for businesses that arguably benefited from their legislative activities. And the 1990s brought the Congressional post office scandal, involving a scheme to launder U.S. post office money, which led to the indictment of Democratic House Ways and Means Comittee chairman Dan Rostenkowski on corruption charges. Charges against Rostenkowski included keeping nonexistent employees on his payroll, using congressional funds to buy gifts for friends, and trading in officially purchased stamps for cash at the House post office.

## THE EFFECT OF LOBBYISTS UNAVOIDABLE

"The problem . . . [is] who pays for politics. Elected officials . . . [cannot] avoid the lobbyists who control, directly or indirectly, much of the money that pays for elections."

—Mark Schmitt, former speechwriter and congressional aide to
Democratic senator Bill Bradley, now a senior fellow at the New
America Foundation, a nonpartisan public policy research group

Mark Schmitt, "The Limits of Limits," *American Prospect,* March 2006, p. 8.

Congressional corruption has continued in recent years. The corruption scandals that resulted in the indictment and resignation of Republican House majority leader Tom DeLay for campaign finance violations and Randy "Duke" Cunningham for outright bribery are only two of the more prominent examples. Former Republican Senate majority leader Bill Frist, too, was linked with numerous ethical and financial trading violations, and Republican congressman Bob Ney pleaded guilty to conspiracy charges in the Abramoff corruption investigation. Meanwhile, Republican House minority whip Roy Blunt has been criticized for his close connections to the tobacco industry. Philip Morris is Blunt's largest political donor; both his wife and his son are Philip Morris lobbyists; and just before an important House vote on

Department of Homeland Security legislation in 2005, Blunt quietly slipped in a provision to benefit Philip Morris.

## Corporate and Lobbying Scandals

Some of the nation's recent corruption scandals have directly implicated major U.S. corporations and their lobbyists and have illustrated the way that corporate money can influence government policies to the great detriment of the public. One early example was the 1980s savings and loan scandal. Savings and loans traditionally had served as community-based businesses that provided home loans, but President Reagan in 1982 signed legislation that removed savings and loans from federal regulation and allowed them to expand into speculative investments and loans that they knew little about. Reagan policy makers and Congress then looked the other way, allowing these businesses to make risky investments and misspend depositors' savings while accepting millions in campaign contributions from their wealthy owners. By the late 1980s, almost a quarter of these savings and loan businesses failed and the entire industry collapsed, creating the largest financial scandal in the nation's history.

### THE SYSTEM IS ROTTEN

"Nothing in the relationship of Enron to the Bush administration or to government regulators has yet been found to have been illegal. Enron simply provides another demonstration of the role of corporate money in the American system. It is the system that is rotten."

—William Pfaff, a journalist and newspaper columnist who has written numerous books about American history and politics

William Pfaff, "The American Problem Is Domination of Politics by Money," *International Herald Tribune,* January 24, 2002. www.commondreams.org/views02/0124-01.htm.

One of the most notorious names associated with the savings and loan corruption was that of Charles Keating, head of a savings and loan business in California, who convinced his customers to invest in worthless junk bonds. He was convicted of fraud, racketeering, and conspiracy in 1993 and sent to prison. Also implicat-

*Charles Keating, right, waits with his attorney at the beginning of his trial for fraud, racketeering, and conspiracy.*

ed were five U.S. senators, three of whom—Alan Cranston, Don Riegle, and Dennis DeConcini—were found to have assisted Keating by meeting with regulators who were investigating his business dealings, in exchange for a total of $1.3 million in campaign contributions. The scandal brought wealth to a few people, but at a terrible public price: U.S. taxpayers were stuck with paying for the industry's federally insured accounts at a cost of over $125 billion.

Even more recently, the George W. Bush administration's close ties to Enron, a Texas energy company, have been under scrutiny. From its founding in 1985 until it grew into America's seventh-largest company, Enron had been a major supporter and friend of the entire Bush family. As Kevin Phillips explains: "It seems clear, counting campaign contributions, consultancies, joint investments, deals, presidential library and inaugural contributions, speech fees and the like, that the Bush family and entourage collected some $8 million to $10 million from Enron over the years. . . . Depending on some still-unclear relationships, it could be as high as $25 million."[23] This support, critics say, helped Enron to influence the top levels of decision making, not only in the first Bush administration, but also when the younger Bush was elected president.

In 2000, for example, incoming president George W. Bush appointed dozens of Enron officials, advisers, and consultants to high-level positions within the new administration. As journalist John Nichols explains, "From Army Secretary Thomas White, a former Enron executive, to Trade Representative Robert Zoellick, formerly on Enron's advisory council, Enron's tentacles have reached throughout the Bush White House, shaping tax, trade, energy and environmental policy."[24] Enron was especially involved in energy policy, meeting numerous times with vice president Dick Cheney and his energy task force. Recommendations made by Enron in an April 2001 memo to Cheney, for example, became part of the administration's energy plan. As Nichols explains, "Seventeen policies sought by Enron or that clearly benefit[ed] the company—including proposals to extend federal control of transmission lines, use federal eminent-domain authority to override state decisions on transmission-line siting, expedite permitting for new energy facilities and limit the use of price controls—were included."[25]

## ABSCAM

The Federal Bureau of Investigation (FBI) is the federal agency charged with investigating political corruption in the United States. The FBI's Web site, in fact, states that corruption is one of the agency's most important priorities. One of the FBI's most famous corruption investigations occurred in 1978, when an FBI sting operation called ABSCAM targeted several members of Congress suspected of political corruption. In the operation, FBI employees posed as Middle Eastern businessmen and offered money to legislators in return for political favors to a nonexistent sheik. Altogether, out of thirty-one officials targeted, six federal legislators—one senator (Democrat Harrison A. Williams from New Jersey) and five members of the House of Representatives (Democrat John Jenrette from South Carolina, Republican Richard Kelly from Florida, Democrat Frank Thompson from New Jersey, and Democrats Raymond Lederer and Michael Myers from Pennsylvania)—were convicted of bribery and conspiracy. Also, one House member (John M. Murphy of New York) was convicted of a lesser charge, and five lesser government officials received criminal sentences.

*The Enron scandal led to numerous calls for reform. This woman is one of many who protested throughout New York City during the 2002 World Economic Forum.*

Enron maintained its close ties with the Bush administration throughout a 2000–2001 energy crisis in California that caused huge jumps in the price of electricity and numerous rolling blackouts for millions of American consumers. During the crisis, despite widespread calls for intervention, the administration refused to investigate complaints about market manipulation by energy companies. Later, evidence clearly showed that Enron had manipulated the market with price-fixing schemes (called names like "Death Star" and "Fat Boy,"), in order to profit from the California crisis. Representative Henry Waxman, a Democratic member of the House Committee on Government Reform, began an investigation in 2003 into Enron's influence with the Bush White House and questioned what he called "the administration's failure to take prompt and effective action to protect Western consumers from price gouging and market manipulation."[26] Vice President Cheney, however, steadfastly refused to turn over the records of his task force or meetings with Enron representatives, and the administration stonewalled the investigation.

When Enron imploded in December 2001, Bush refused Enron a federal bailout, but critics charge that Bush helped to ease government regulations, allowing the energy company to undertake speculative business ventures that led to massive fraud. As journalist Sam Parry charges:

> Bush pitched in as governor and president whenever the energy trader wanted easier regulations within the U.S. or to have U.S. taxpayers foot the bill for loan guarantees or risk insurance for Enron's overseas ventures. . . . Enron wouldn't have . . . [been] in a position for its executives to make off with hundreds of millions of dollars while leaving small investors and low-level employees to take the fall— without years of assistance from George W. Bush.[27]

These and other examples, critics claim, show that America's top elected officials are no longer working for the good of ordinary people, but instead doing the bidding of their wealthy and corporate donors. As journalist Bill Moyers recently argued:

> Look back at the bulk of legislation passed by Congress in the past decade: an energy bill that gives oil companies huge tax breaks at the same time that ExxonMobil has just posted $36.13 billion in profits and our gasoline and home heating bills are at an all-time high; a bankruptcy "reform" bill written by credit card companies to make it harder for poor debtors to escape the burdens of divorce or medical

# Political Scandals in San Diego

Corruption is not limited to the federal level. Over the years, political corruption scandals have also erupted at state and local government levels. One recent example is a scandal called Strippergate in San Diego, California. In August 2003, three city councilmen—Michael Zucchet, Ralph Inzunza, and Charles Lewis—were charged with accepting $34,500 in campaign contributions from the owner of a local club in exchange for help changing a city ordinance that benefited the business. Lewis died before the trial, but in July 2005 both Inzunza and Zucchet were convicted (Zucchet's conviction was later overturned). Ironically, just days before the verdict, Zucchet replaced Mayor Dick Murphy, who resigned July 15, 2005, amid another scandal involving a deficit of $1.43 billion in the city's pension fund. The U.S. Attorney's office and the Securities and Exchange Commission are investigating the pension matter. In August 2006, however, a firm hired by the city found that city officials, including five council members still in office, negligently failed to catch inaccuracies in bond disclosures linked to the pension deficit.

catastrophe; the deregulation of the banking, securities and insurance sectors, which brought on rampant corporate malfeasance [wrongdoing] and greed and the destruction of the retirement plans of millions of small investors; the deregulation of the telecommunications sector, which led to cable industry price-gouging and an undermining of news coverage; protection for rampant overpricing of pharmaceutical drugs; and the blocking of even the mildest attempt to prevent American corporations from dodging an estimated $50 billion in annual taxes by opening a P.O. box in an off-shore tax haven like the Cayman Islands.[28]

Despite its status as the largest and most open democracy in the world, the United States is still mired in corruption, much of it directly related to the enormous amounts of money flowing into its election system.

# CHAPTER 4

# POLITICAL CORRUPTION AROUND THE WORLD

Although many experts conclude that America leads democratic countries in the degree of election financing corruption, this and other forms of corruption are also rampant in other parts of the world. Indeed, as economics scholar Robert Klitgaard explains, "Corruption exists everywhere, in private as well as public sectors, in rich countries and poor."[29] Much of the focus recently has been on developing countries, which often lack even the most basic anticorruption laws. However, many industrialized, democratic nations face election financing dilemmas similar to those that plague the U.S. government. In recent years of increasing globalization, the world has also witnessed corruption scandals at international levels.

## Corruption in Developing Countries

According to Transparency International (TI), which has compiled global rankings of corruption, 72 of 158 nations monitored by the group in 2005 are corrupt. Some of the most corrupt countries in the world are those with high levels of poverty, political instability, few political freedoms, and weak legal and financial institutions—characteristics that typically define poorer, developing nations. In fact, TI has named ten developing nations, many of them African countries, as the world's most corrupt nations: Bangladesh, Chad, Haiti, Myanmar, Turkmenistan, Ivory Coast, Equatorial Guinea, Nigeria, Angola, and Democratic Republic of Congo. Other poor and less developed regions, however, such as Asia, Latin America, and eastern Europe, have also developed reputations for high levels of corruption. Scandinavian countries—Iceland, Finland, Denmark, Sweden, and Norway—along with

New Zealand, Singapore, Australia, Austria, and Switzerland top the list as the ten least corrupt countries.

Developing countries with large oil industries seem to be some of the most prone to corruption. As TI chairman Peter Eigen explains: "Oil-rich Angola, Azerbaijan, Chad, Ecuador, Indonesia, Iran, Iraq, Kazakhstan, Libya, Nigeria, Russia, Sudan, Venezuela and Yemen all have extremely low scores. . . . In these countries, public contracting in the oil sector is plagued by revenues vanishing into

*An Indonesian high school student holds up a sign during an anticorruption demonstration. Corruption is a serious problem in many developing nations.*

the pockets of Western oil executives, middlemen and local officials."[30] Indeed, according to many experts, the presence of valuable natural resources such as oil usually makes life worse for people in developing countries, not better. Battles over these valuable resources often lead to greater political instability and strife, dictatorial or unrepresentative government, as well as widespread corruption.

## THE IMPACT OF CORRUPTION

"The true impact of corruption is now widely acknowledged: corruption distorts markets and competition, breeds cynicism among citizens, undermines the rule of law, damages government legitimacy, and corrodes the integrity of the private sector. It is also a major barrier to international development—systemic misappropriation by kleptocratic governments harms the poor."
—Ben W. Heineman Jr., a senior fellow at Harvard's Belfer Center for Science and International Affairs, and Fritz Heimann, cofounder of the corruption watchdog group Transparency International

Ben W. Heineman Jr. and Fritz Heimann, "The Long War Against Corruption," *Foreign Affairs*, May/June 2006.

Corruption in developing nations typically involves flagrantly corrupt actions by high-level government officials. In fact, bribery and kickbacks on government contracts are commonplace in many developing countries, and quite a few presidents have been accused of embezzling millions or even billions of public funds from their countries. The poor and most vulnerable citizens pay the biggest price for corruption because such practices divert scarce government resources away from legitimate public needs, such as social programs, education, and health care. This, in turn, often results in the perpetuation of poverty and disease, and in ineffective, repressive governments that only benefit a wealthy few. As international economic researcher Kimberly Ann Elliott explains, "Corruption may stabilize a political situation that is repressive and unjust, in which all but a wealthy elite lack the resources to protect themselves from exploitation."[31]

Corruption is also particularly damaging for the economies of developing nations. According to international agencies such as the World Bank and the International Monetary Fund (IMF), corruption in weak economies reduces international developmental aid and slows economic growth by scaring away investors and donors. As Pino Arlacchi, Executive Director of the UN Office for Drug Control and Crime Prevention, explains, "Obviously, it is wiser to invest in countries with more transparency, independent and well-regulated banks and strong court systems."[32] In a recent World Bank survey, representatives from more than sixty developing nations agreed that corruption was the main obstacle to economic development and growth. Economist Shang-Jin Wei explains:

> For international investors, having to pay bribes and deal with official extortion is equivalent to facing an extra tax. Some foreign firms may have obtained business because of the bribes they paid. But for every dollar of business that these firms obtain, the country loses multiple dollars of potential foreign investment. My research estimates that an increase in the host country corruption from a low level such as that in Singapore to a higher level, such as that in Mexico, has the same negative effect on inward foreign direct investment (FDI) as raising the corporate tax rate by fifty percentage points. This negative impact is akin to a tax on firms in that it discourages investment. But, unlike a tax, corruption generates no tax revenue for the government.[33]

In Latin America, for example, corruption has long been widespread and is increasingly seen as a major cause of the region's stagnant economic growth and persistent poverty. Latin democracies created following several bitter civil wars in the 1980s have in recent years been threatened by a host of corruption scandals implicating high-level officials. Nicaragua has one of the worst corruption records. After convicting former president Arnoldo Alemán for diverting over $100 million in government funds into his party's election campaign, the country faced another corruption scandal in 2004 when Nicaragua's comptroller's

# Political Corruption in Mexico

Experts say Mexico has many advantages, such as oil, agriculture, and tourism, that could make it a very prosperous country, but it fails to succeed largely because of a long history of government corruption. In fact, corruption is so pervasive in Mexico that it takes a bribe to government officials to do just about anything—open a business, obtain a driver's license, or apply for public services. Mexican officials have estimated that this corruption steals as much as 9 percent annually from the country's gross domestic product, the nation's total yearly output of goods and services. Corruption essentially acts as a hidden tax that slows the country's economic growth and saps its vitality. When Vicente Fox was elected president in 2000, many people hoped he would clean up Mexican corruption. Fox appointed an anticorruption czar and helped to pass a landmark transparency law designed to give citizens greater access to public records. Most commentators, however, agree that Fox has failed to produce significant reforms. His political coalition, Alliance for Change, was

fined nearly $50 million by election authorities in 2003 for campaign finance violations that included accepting millions in undisclosed donations.

*When Vicente Fox was elected president of Mexico, there were high hopes that he would curb corruption.*

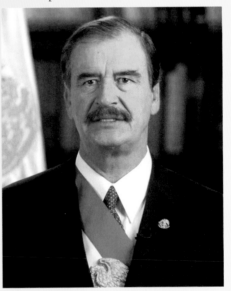

office called for the impeachment of Alemán's successor and self-proclaimed anticorruption leader, President Enrique Bolaños, on grounds that he failed to disclose the origin of $7 million used in his 2001 presidential campaign.

Costa Rica has similar problems. Ex-president Rafael Ángel Calderón Fournier was charged with accepting a corporate kickback of $440,500 during his 1990–1994 presidency. And ex-president Miguel Ángel Rodríguez was recently forced to resign as secretary general of the Organization of American States after he was arrested on charges that he accepted kickbacks from a French telecom corporation during his 1998–2002 presidential term. Costa Rica's current president, Abel Pacheco, is suspected of taking campaign donations from foreign businesses, a violation of Costa Rican campaign finance laws.

High-level corruption has affected numerous other Latin countries as well. Honduran former president Rafael Callejas is suspected of misappropriating as much as $20 million of government funds; Guatemalan former president Alfonso Portillo is suspected of stealing $3.7 million from the country's coffers; and ex-Chilean leader General Augusto Pinochet, before his death, was charged with embezzling and stashing millions of dollars of government funds in U.S. and offshore bank accounts. Meanwhile, in Brazil, leaders from the country's governing Workers Party are under investigation for diverting funds from state-owned banks and other entities to bribe legislators for their support for government-sponsored initiatives in Congress. Across Latin America, according to the Inter-American Development Bank, corruption eats up as much as 20 percent of funds earmarked for government projects and accounts for the loss of 10 percent of gross national product, the measure of countries' economic output and health.

Often too, government corruption becomes intimately linked with criminal

*Nicaragua has been threatened by numerous corruption scandals. President Enrique Bolaños was impeached for failing to disclose money.*

*Former president of Costa Rica Miguel Ángel Rodríguez faced corruption charges in 2005.*

activity. In many formerly Communist parts of eastern and southern Europe, for example, the breakdown of communism in the late 1980s caused a scramble for power and government assets that has resulted in a wave of crime and corruption. Such is the case in Bosnia, once part of Communist Yugoslavia, where power struggles and ethnic tensions resulted in a war that began in 1992. During the war, criminal gangs developed, black markets flourished, and criminal elements managed to loot much of the country's wealth as well as the aid that poured in from other countries. A 1995 peace accord ended the fighting, but crime and corruption have persisted and made Bosnia's recovery from war very difficult. In 1999, for example, a massive corruption scandal ensued when it was revealed that $2.1 billion in UN relief was stolen by Bosnia's leaders, many of whom have links to criminal organizations. As TI spokesperson Srdjan Blagovcanin explains: "The reason for the stagnation of the fight against corruption in Bosnia is ties of the political elite with organised crime. . . . It is not a secret in Bosnia that a very big number of politicians have very close connections with people from the other side of the law."[34]

## Corruption Scandals in the Industrialized World

Even the world's most developed nations, however, continue to struggle with the problem of corruption. The economic effects may be less severe in richer countries than in poorer countries, but corruption still acts as an insidious, negative force that threatens government stability and people's well-being. As Kimberly Ann Elliott explains:

> Even in rich countries diverted resources will not be available for improving living standards. Corruption also tends to exacerbate income inequalities by increasing the power of those willing and able to pay bribes to the detriment of those who cannot. . . . Finally, corruption can undermine politcal legitimacy in industrialized democracies as well as in developing ones by alienating the citizenry from its political leadership and making effective government more difficult.[35]

## CORRUPTION IN POOR COUNTRIES

"In poor countries, corruption may lower economic growth, impede economic development, and undermine political legitimacy, consequences that in turn exacerbate poverty and political instability."

—Kimberly Ann Elliott, a research fellow at the Institute for International Economics, a private, nonprofit, nonpartisan research institution devoted to the study of international economic policy

Kimberly Ann Elliott, ed., *Corruption and the Global Economy.* Washington, DC: Institute for International Economics, 1997, p. 1.

This destabilizing effect of corruption was recently seen in Canada, historically one of the world's least corrupt and most democratic countries. There, a major corruption scandal helped to upset the ruling Liberal Party in the country's 2006 national elections. The scandal, called Sponsorgate, resulted from revelations of corruption in the operation of a program set up in French-speaking Quebec to publicize the national government's contributions to Quebec province to counter the local government's promotion of Quebec sovereignty. Investigations showed favoritism in the distribution of $100 million in public funds, benefiting the Liberal Party. Eventually, the scandal was linked with the prime minister's office, helping to ensure a win by the rival Conservative Party in early 2006.

A number of European democracies have also faced major scandals in recent decades. France, for example, has been plagued by a string of political scandals that have involved illegal political fund-raising by some of its most elite leaders. In the 1990s a series of scandals led to the conviction of numerous businessmen and politicians for embezzling taxpayer money to bankroll political parties. One of these was former prime minister Alain Juppé, who was convicted for permitting party workers to be paid by Paris's city hall. Even Jacques Chirac, the current president, has been linked to illegal kickbacks and embezzlement schemes.

## CORRUPTION UNCHECKED

"Corruption may have the most deleterious effects in countries in transition, such as Russia, where, left unchecked, it could under-mine support for democracy and a market economy."

—Kimberly Ann Elliott, a research fellow at the Institute for International Economics, a private, nonprofit, nonpartisan research institution devoted to the study of international economic policy

Kimberly Ann Elliott, ed., *Corruption and the Global Economy.* Washington, DC: Institute for International Economics, 1997, p. 2.

The most recent French political scandal, called the Clearstream affair, has been compared to America's Watergate scandal. It began with an investigation of possible kickbacks asso-ciated with the 1991 sale of six French warships to Taiwan. In 2004 judges investigating the matter received an anonymous list of foreign bank accounts linked to various politicians, including Nicolas Sarkozy, France's interior minister and the chief rival of French prime minister Dominique de Villepin. The list itself, however, was found to be fraudulent, and subsequent evidence from a retired government spy has suggested that Prime Minister de Villepin and President Chirac may have created the list as part of a political smear campaign against Sarkozy.

# Corruption in International Construction Projects

Experts say global corruption is especially damaging in the construction sector. A 2005 report by Transparency International (TI) on this problem found that when bribes and other forms of corruption infect large-scale public infrastructure projects (such as roads, bridges, and rail lines), the resulting projects are often overpriced, badly constructed, and built in areas that can damage the environment or even cost human lives. As TI chairman Peter Eigen explained:

> Corrupt contracting processes leave developing countries saddled with sub-standard infrastructure and excessive debt. . . . Corruption raises the cost and lowers the quality of infrastructure. But the cost of corruption is also felt in lost lives. The damage caused by natural disasters such as earthquakes is magnified in places where inspectors have been bribed to ignore building and planning regulations. . . . Corruption can also have disastrous environmental consequences—the Yacyretá dam in Argentina, the Bataan nuclear power plant in the Philippines and the Bujagali dam in Uganda have all been subject to allegations of the improper diversion of money.

Quoted in Transparency International, "Press Release: A World Built on Bribes?" March 16, 2005. http://www.transparency.org/pressreleases_archive/2005/2005.03.16.gcr_relaunch.html.

Even Germany, which once had a good reputation as a relatively uncorrupt nation, has encountered serious corruption problems. In one 1993 scandal, for example, Premier Werner Munch, the head of the eastern state of Saxony-Anhalt, resigned after he and three of his ministers were found to have taken about six hundred thousand dollars in undisclosed income from the government. A number of other scandals involved government officials taking bribes from companies seeking public construction or service contracts. Still another massive scandal in the late 1990s rocked then chancellor Helmut Kohl's Christian Democratic Party and revealed that party political activities were financed by secret slush accounts funded by huge bribes paid by foreign arms dealers and oil corporations. According to reports, one deal directly involved former chancellor Helmut Kohl and the late French president François Mitterrand in the sale of a German refinery (Leuna) to France's giant oil corporation, Elf Aquitaine. Elf executives testified that the company paid 40 million euros as a kickback to Christian Democrat politicians for arranging the deal.

Other European countries, too, have experienced their share of corruption scandals. Silvio Berlusconi, Italian billionaire and Italy's prime minister until May 2006, has been accused of embezzlement, tax fraud, and trying to bribe a judge to stop a rival company from taking over a state-owned food group in the 1980s.

*Silvio Berlusconi, top, former prime minister of Italy, is facing several corruption charges. British prime minister Tony Blair has been criticized for corruption scandals.*

Even the highly reputed British prime minister Tony Blair has come under criticism—for helping an Indian steel tycoon who is a major contributor to Blair's Labour Party, and for recommending four of Britain's richest men for peerages, or nobility titles, after they made million-dollar loans to the Labour Party before the last election.

Notably, many of the corruption scandals in European countries have involved campaign finance motivations, the same type of corruption problem currently faced by the United States. Some commentators attribute this to the fact that European elections are becoming more Americanized—that is, focused primarily on personalities and appearances rather than on issues and requiring ever larger amounts of campaign money for expensive television ad campaigns. Another theory is that Europe is ripe for graft, patronage, and other forms of corruption because of its large social welfare system and the large number of political appointees. Others blame modern economic trends. Privatization, for example, encourages governments to contract with private companies for the provision of public services or utilities. Critics say this encourages bribery from companies competing to win these lucrative deals and can lead to situations in which government officials can hand out or influence hiring for high-paying jobs in these companies, but without the scrutiny that would come if the jobs were with the government.

Regardless of the motivation, corruption is causing disillusionment and cynicism about politics, even in some of the world's strongest democracies. In some cases, this takes the form of voters ousting the political party in power in favor of the opposition, as happened in Canada in 2006. In other countries, public disgust over corruption scandals has resulted in protest votes for fringe candidates. This occurred in France's 2002 elections, when 17 percent of the electorate voted for far-right candidate Jean-Marie Le Pen, rattling the country's political establishment. In the United States, where there are only two main political parties, public apathy has increasingly caused citizens to refrain from voting completely. The 1996 U.S. presidential election, for example, produced the lowest voter turnout since 1924, with only 49.1 percent of the voting-age population casting votes. Subsequent presidential elections in 2000 and 2004 fared only slightly better, with turnouts of 51.3 percent and 55.4 percent, respectively. Mid-term congressional elections typically produce even more abysmally low voter turnouts, but the number of voters in the 1998 congressional elections dropped to a new low of only 36 percent of eligible voters. As journalist Elizabeth Drew explains, this turnout was "lower than that for any midterm elections since 1942."[36]

## Globalization and Corruption

The recent trend of globalization and increased trade spurred by technological advances in communication and transportation has only increased the opportunities for corruption. Today, large multinational corporations frequently trade with foreign governments or companies around the world, often in places where corruption is deeply entrenched. In order to gain export and other contracts with these countries, many corporations based in richer nations have routinely bribed foreign leaders and officials of developing countries, even though such practices are prohibited in their home countries. At the same time, a new international system of finance, which allows funds to be quickly moved from one country to another, makes illegal funds more difficult to track and much easier to launder. Embezzlers or bribe takers now can electronically transfer large amounts of cash to confidential accounts or legitimate businesses in other countries. The result has been an escalation of corruption beyond national borders to the transnational or international level.

Some experts hold rich countries responsible for this growing problem of global corruption. As Professor Robert Neild from Trinity College, Cambridge University, writes, "Rich countries and their agencies . . . commonly have been and are accomplices in corruption abroad, encouraging it by their actions rather than impeding it."[37] Indeed, although the United States has banned foreign bribery since the 1977 Foreign Corrupt Practices Act, a number of other industrialized countries that have historically regulated corruption at home have nevertheless permitted their corporations to offer bribes overseas. As corruption expert Susan Hawley explains: "Until recently, bribery was seen as a normal business practice. Many countries including France, Germany and the UK treated bribes as legitimate business expenses which could be claimed for tax deduction purposes."[38]

## SUCCESS IN SPITE OF CORRUPTION

"It is possible . . . to find examples of places that have done well [economically] in spite of corruption, but hard to think of anywhere that has done well because of it!"

—Shang-Jin Wei, an economist and senior fellow at the Brookings Institution, a private nonprofit public policy research organization

Quoted in Brookings Institution, "Corruption in Developing Countries," March 12, 2003. www.brookings.edu/views/speeches/wei/20030312.htm.

This system, experts say, allowed rich countries and their corporations more easily to exploit developing nations for their natural resources (such as deposits of oil, copper, gold, and diamonds) and gain large profits. At the same time, however, the system has served to keep corrupt rulers in power in poor countries and allowed them to embezzle billions of dollars of public money that otherwise could have been used for alleviating poverty and other problems faced by people in those developing regions. In fact, according to Susan Hawley, "These bribes are conservatively estimated to run to US$80 billion a year—roughly the amount that the UN estimates is needed to eradicate global poverty."[39]

In addition to taking billions away from the poor, this phenomenon of global corruption endangers the stability of the world economy and international political relations. Just as at the national level, corruption on a wider scale distorts the global economic system in ways that inhibit trade and growth. As globalization experts Patrick Glynn, Stephen J. Kobrin, and Moisés Naím explain:

Widespread corruption threatens the very basis of an open, multilateral world economy. Multilateralism depends on trust and a belief that others will play by the rules. The tendency to cheat . . . is a constant threat to the international economic system. Tolerance of corruption tilts the playing field—against firms (and countries) that will not or cannot engage in bribes and other corrupt practices. Corruption distorts competition and may reduce gains from free flows of trade and investment.[40]

## Corruption in International Organizations

Global corruption has also infected international organizations charged with distributing international aid and assistance. A clear example of this was seen when an international scandal erupted involving the Oil for Food program, a UN plan to aid Iraqi citizens during a period when international economic sanctions were

*An Iraqi woman and her baby wait to receive food through a rationing program. The now-defunct UN Oil for Food program was designed to provide similar assistance, but was marred by extensive corruption.*

imposed to demilitarize Iraq during Saddam Hussein's rule. The program, which lasted from 1995 to 2003, created an exception to the sanctions that allowed Iraq to sell a total of $65 billion of oil on the world market to pay for food, medicine, and other humanitarian items needed by the Iraqi people. However, the program reportedly suffered from widespread corruption throughout its operation. Saddam Hussein, by offering bribes, smuggling shipments of oil, and demanding kickbacks from companies with whom he contracted, managed to skim at least $10 billion in profits from the program, at a cost of further suffering by the Iraqi people. Subsequent investigations have implicated numerous corporations, entire governments (such as nearby Jordan), as well as high-level UN officials, including Benon Sevan, head of the Oil for Food program.

International financial institutions such as the World Bank and the IMF have also been criticized for corruption. Such charges are significant because these institutions finance economic development projects on a global scale; the World Bank doles out roughly $45 billion to $50 billion in financing each year, and IMF loans more than double that amount. Critics charge that many of the development projects go to favored firms because of corporate lobbying activities and that institutional monitoring and audit systems have been weak, allowing funds to be misappropriated or siphoned off by corrupt officials. Allegations have arisen, for example, that funds from IMF loans to Russia were stolen by Russian elites and deposited in Western banks; Russian president Boris Yeltsin reportedly spent $5 million of international funds to finance his reelection campaign in 1996. Because of concerns about corruption, the World Bank has recently suspended a number of loans, including contracts with Chad, Kenya, Democratic Republic of the Congo, India, Bangladesh, Uzbekistan, Yemen, and Argentina.

As the above examples illustrate, corruption is pervasive around the world. Some commentators despair at the huge scope of the problem and worry that greed will always motivate practices such as bribery and influence peddling. Despite the daunting obstacles, however, there is a movement for change, as people become aware of corruption and demand reforms.

# EFFORTS TO CURB POLITICAL CORRUPTION

The publicity surrounding recent national and international corruption scandals has helped to inspire a wave of anticorruption efforts around the world. Since the 1990s, a series of international initiatives has been adopted that calls for reforms in the way that companies do business with foreign partners. Some countries, too, have adopted and enforced stricter anticorruption and campaign finance laws. Anticorruption laws and treaties, however, are often difficult to achieve because of public cynicism and resistance to change from those in power. Nevertheless, advocates for reform are continuing their fight for anticorruption action to curb the influence of money in elections and government, both in the United States and internationally.

## The Anticorruption Movement

Today, people around the world are becoming more aware of the dangers and costs of corruption. As corruption experts Patrick Glynn, Stephen J. Kobrin, and Moisés Naím write:

> There have been both real and perceived increases in corrupt activity in various countries. In some regions, systemic political change has weakened or destroyed social, political, and legal institutions, opening the way to new abuses. Elsewhere, political and economic liberalization has simply exposed corruption that was once hidden. But almost everywhere, we observe a marked decrease in the willingness of the public to tolerate corrupt practices by their political leaders and economic elites.[41]

Many experts attribute this new awareness largely to the end of the Cold War, the standoff between the United States and the Soviet Union that occupied much of the twentieth century. During the Cold War, the focus was largely on holding the line against communism, and the United States and other Western democracies formed relationships with developing nations largely without regard to whether their governments were corrupt. Western governments, as Robert Neild explains,

> were motivated, in part at least, by the view . . . that the West's supplies of raw materials and oil were threatened by communist intrusion into Third World countries. A feeling of vulnerability was understandable. The Soviet

*In the wake of numerous corruption scandals, there has been a wave of anticorruption efforts around the world.*

Union . . . was largely self-sufficient . . . ; the West, in need of increasing supplies for its growing industrial production, depended heavily on imports from Third World countries.[42]

As a result, many corrupt dictators were kept in power for decades with Western arms and loans. After the fall of communism and the breakup of the Soviet Union in 1991, this Cold War dynamic vanished, and a string of peaceful revolutions brought democratic governments to eastern Europe, Asia, and Latin America. Suddenly, people felt freer to challenge often-corrupt dictatorships and demand more open and honest governments.

## ACCEPTING CORRUPTION

"Nearly half of the world's nations are corrupt, and many of them aren't doing very much about it at all."
—David A. Andelman, an executive editor at *Forbes*,
a business and financial magazine

David A. Andelman, "A Stewpot of Corruption," *Forbes*, February 2, 2006. www.forbes.com/2006/02/03/corrupt-nations-world-cx_daa_0206caphosp.html.

The increase in international trade in this post–Cold War period also contributed to the concerns about corruption. Today, as Glynn, Kobrin, and Naím explain, "The security of one nation can be radically affected by purely domestic developments in a seemingly distant state."[43] This increased economic interconnectedness among nations made all nations more vulnerable to negative forces such as corruption, motivating international efforts to reduce its economic risks and costs.

## International Reforms and Proposals

In the 1990s, in fact, corruption emerged as a truly global issue. Although international organizations such as the UN, the World Bank, and the IMF had ignored corruption for many years, this changed in 1996 when James Wolfensohn, then the World Bank president, challenged that indifference in a speech in which he described the "cancer of corruption"[44] and its effects on the global economy. Since then, a blitz of activity has been undertaken to seek international solutions to the problems of bribery, extortion, and similar practices. As corruption experts Ben W. Heineman Jr. and Fritz Heimann explain:

> International organizations, including the Organization for Economic Cooperation and Development (OECD) and the UN, have adopted conventions requiring that their members enact laws prohibiting bribery and extortion. International financial agencies, notably the World Bank, have announced programs aimed at ensuring fair and open contracting for their projects and stopping misappropriation by government officials. Most nations have enacted some type of anticorruption law. International business groups have promulgated model codes of behavior, and multinational corporations (MNCs) now claim to be implementing antibribery programs. The leading nongovernmental organization (NGO) in this area, Transparency International, has conducted analysis and advocacy through chapters in over 90 nations. The international media report instances of corruption in high places virtually every day (often at great risk).[45]

The World Bank, for example, adopted a comprehensive anticorruption program in 1997 that includes both prohibitions against bribery in World Bank–financed projects and assistance to governments to promote anticorruption reforms. In 1999 the World Bank created a unit to investigate instances of corruption. This unit, called the Department of Institutional Integrity, employs twenty-two investigators and spends about $10 million annually to look into allegations of corruption in countries to which it provides development loans. Since its creation, the department has investigated almost two thousand corruption cases. Similar efforts are being undertaken at the IMF and other international lending agencies.

The first big achievement of the international reform movement, however, was the Convention on Combating Bribery of Foreign Public Officials, a treaty that prohibits the use of bribes

*The headquarters of the World Bank is located in Washington, D.C.*

by companies seeking to win contracts in foreign countries. The treaty was adopted in 1997 by the Organization for Economic Cooperation and Development (OECD), an international agency made up of representatives from thirty member countries that supports programs for trade and development. All thirty OECD countries signed and ratified the treaty, along with seven non-OECD countries that participated voluntarily.

The treaty developed from a U.S. ban on foreign bribes adopted in the Foreign Corrupt Practices Act of 1977, but other countries did not immediately follow America's lead. Instead, as anticorruption advocates John Brademas and Fritz Heimann point out, "The [U.S.] act was derided as misguided American moralism."[46] Other countries, therefore, continued to allow their multinational corporations to use bribes to win foreign contracts, sometimes even allowing companies to take tax deductions for the bribes. The OECD treaty finally changed this situation twenty years later by getting other developed nations to adopt a bribery ban. Experts say enforcing this treaty is vitally important because its signatories are industrialized countries that are home to most of the world's multinational corporations responsible for global trading.

Anticorruption initiatives have also been adopted by three regional organizations—the Council of Europe, the Organization of American States, and the African Union. In addition, an anticorruption plan launched by the Asian Development Bank has been signed by twenty-five Asian countries, and a similar program is being promoted by developed countries in the Middle East and North Africa.

## A LOSING BATTLE

"The reality of fighting corruption . . . has been a disillusioning experience in most of the developing world."

—Donald Greenlees, reporter for the *International Herald Tribune* newspaper

Donald Greenlees, "Anti-corruption Fight Stalled," *International Herald Tribune,* May 31, 2006.

The most recent and perhaps most promising international treaty on corruption is the UN Convention Against Corruption (UNCAC), a treaty adopted by the UN General Assembly in 2003 with 140 signatories. The treaty is much broader than the OECD treaty and includes provisions on corruption prevention, criminalization, international cooperation, and asset recovery. Also, unlike the OECD convention, UNCAC covers both industrialized and less developed countries, creating the possibility of a worldwide anticorruption program. UNCAC only recently became effective, in December 2005.

# Countries That Have Ratified the UN Convention Against Corruption

A total of 140 countries have signed the UN Convention Against Corruption. The countries listed below have also ratified the document.

| Country | Date | Country | Date |
|---|---|---|---|
| Albania | May 25, 2006 | Lithuania | Dec. 21, 2006 |
| Algeria | Aug. 25, 2004 | Madagascar | Sep. 22, 2004 |
| Angola | Aug. 29, 2006 | Mauritius | Dec. 15, 2004 |
| Argentina | Aug. 28, 2006 | Mexico | Jul. 20, 2004 |
| Armenia | Mar. 8, 2007 | Mongolia | Jan. 11, 2006 |
| Australia | Dec. 7, 2005 | Namibia | Aug. 3, 2004 |
| Austria | Jan. 11, 2006 | Nicaragua | Feb. 15, 2006 |
| Azerbaijan | Nov. 1, 2005 | Nigeria | Dec. 14, 2004 |
| Belarus | Feb. 17, 2005 | Norway | Jun. 29, 2006 |
| Benin | Oct. 14, 2004 | Panama | Sep. 23, 2005 |
| Bolivia | Dec. 5, 2005 | Paraguay | Jun. 1, 2005 |
| Bosnia and Herzegovina | Oct. 26, 2006 | Peru | Nov. 16, 2004 |
| Brazil | Jun. 15, 2005 | Philippines | Nov. 8, 2006 |
| Bulgaria | Sep. 20, 2006 | Poland | Sep. 16, 2006 |
| Burkina Faso | Oct. 10, 2006 | Qatar | Jan. 30, 2007 |
| Cameroon | Feb. 6, 2006 | Romania | Nov. 2, 2004 |
| Central African Republic | Oct. 6, 2006 | Russian Federation | May 9, 2006 |
| Chile | Sep. 13, 2006 | Rwanda | Oct. 4, 2006 |
| China | Jan. 13, 2006 | Sao Tome and Principe | Apr. 12, 2006 |
| Colombia | Oct. 27, 2006 | Senegal | Nov. 16, 2005 |
| Costa Rica | Mar. 21, 2007 | Serbia | Dec. 20, 2005 |
| Croatia | Apr. 24, 2005 | Seychelles | Mar. 16, 2006 |
| Cuba | Feb. 9, 2007 | Sierra Leone | Sep. 30, 2004 |
| Denmark | Dec. 26, 2006 | Slovakia | Jun. 1, 2006 |
| Djibouti | Apr. 20, 2005 | South Africa | Nov. 22, 2004 |
| Dominican Republic | Oct. 26, 2006 | Spain | Jun. 19, 2006 |
| Ecuador | Sep. 15, 2005 | Sri Lanka | Mar. 31, 2004 |
| Egypt | Feb. 25, 2005 | Togo | Jul. 6, 2005 |
| El Salvador | Jul. 1, 2004 | Trinidad and Tobago | May 31, 2006 |
| France | Jul. 11, 2005 | Turkey | Nov. 9, 2006 |
| Guatemala | Nov. 3, 2006 | Uganda | Sep. 9, 2004 |
| Honduras | May 23, 2005 | United Arab Emirates | Feb. 22, 2006 |
| Hungary | Apr. 19, 2005 | United Kingdom of Great Britain and Northern Ireland | Feb. 9, 2006 |
| Indonesia | Sep. 19, 2006 | United Republic of Tanzania | May 25, 2005 |
| Jordan | Feb. 24, 2005 | United States of America | Oct. 30, 2006 |
| Kenya | Dec. 9, 2003 | Uruguay | Jan. 10, 2007 |
| Kuwait | Feb. 16, 2007 | Yemen | Nov. 7, 2005 |
| Kyrgyzstan | Sep. 16, 2005 | Zimbabwe | Mar. 8, 2007 |
| Latvia | Jan. 4, 2006 | | |
| Lesotho | Sep. 16, 2005 | | |
| Libyan Arab Jamahiriya | Jun. 7, 2005 | | |

Source: "United Nations Convention Against Corruption," United Nations Office on Drugs and Crime. www.unodc.org/unodc/crime_signatures_corruption.html.

## The Success of International Reforms

The ultimate success of UNCAC, the OECD treaty, and other initiatives will depend largely on the enforcement efforts of each individual country, however, and so far these international efforts have had a very limited effect. As of March 2005, for example, a TI report indicated that only fifteen of the nations signing the OECD treaty have begun to enforce anticorruption measures, and only four countries (the United States, France, South Korea, and Spain) have brought more than one prosecution. Also, as of the summer of 2006, only forty-nine countries have ratified the UNCAC—the first step toward complying with treaty requirements. In Asia, for example, almost all countries signed the treaty, but only China and Sri Lanka have ratified it so far. Without ratification by most of the world's countries, the treaty will have limited effect.

Recent World Bank reports confirm that corruption has remained an intractable problem, especially in developing countries.

# The 2005 Corruption Perception Index

Transparency International (TI), the international anticorruption group, issues an annual report that ranks countries according to the degree of corruption among public officials and politicians. The ranking is based on corruption-related data in expert surveys carried out by a variety of institutions as well as the views of local experts and businesspeople and analysts around the world. In 2005, TI found that corruption had increased in countries such as Costa Rica, Gabon, Nepal, Papua New Guinea, Russia, Seychelles, Sri Lanka, Suriname, Trinidad and Tobago, and Uruguay. Other countries, however, including Estonia, France, Japan, Jordan, Kazakhstan, Nigeria, Qatar, Taiwan, and Turkey, had made improvements. To reduce corruption, TI recommends that developing countries increase resources for anticorruption efforts and provide for more public access to government information, while richer countries should increase their foreign aid and support for anticorruption reforms. All countries, TI says, should promote anticorruption and good governance efforts and implement the UN Convention Against Corruption and other anticorruption treaties.

The World Bank has monitored the effectiveness of governments since 1996, and it ranks 209 countries according to factors such as their anticorruption efforts, the strength of their legal systems, and improvements to government accountability and press freedom. The data collected by this program show that the efforts to fight corruption have failed in most developing countries. A few countries, such as Indonesia, have made some progress, while others, including South Korea, Vietnam, the Philippines, and Malaysia, have actually regressed and become more corrupt. The levels of corruption in a vast majority of other developing nations, the report found, have remained about the same for the last ten years. As Daniel Kaufman, the director of global programs at the World Bank, explains: "There has been no global improvement on average. . . . It is quite sobering. The average quality of governance worldwide has remained stagnant."[47]

## The Struggle for Reform in the United States

Anticorruption efforts have also faced numerous obstacles in developed nations, even in the United States. Although America has fewer problems with outright bribery and similar forms of corruption than in the past, it still has a campaign finance system that some have described as "more loophole than law."[48] Indeed, no major campaign finance reforms have been enacted since the landmark 1974 Federal Election Campaign Act legislation. Many critics attribute this lack of reform to a reluctance by incumbents from both parties to change a system that benefits them. By using the loopholes in the system, incumbents can amass huge sums of money that virtually guarantee their reelection. As Brown University political science professor Darrell M. West puts it: "Washington's dirty little secret about campaign finance is that the major players are happy with things as they are. Incumbents do very well under contemporary rules. In recent elections, more than 90 percent of the men and women who have sought reelection to Congress have won."[49]

Sadly, the U.S. public's cynical view of politicians as corrupt only helps ensure the status quo. As West argues, "The people have become so desensitized to allegations of financial misdeeds that they assume little can be done about the problem."[50] The media often contribute to this inaction by focusing on sensational news stories, such as small-time bribery scandals, and then failing to explore the deeper problem of systemic campaign finance corruption.

After years of failed attempts, however, Congress finally mustered the votes in 2002 to pass one significant reform—the Bipartisan Campaign Reform Act (BCRA), a law that prohibited soft money donations to political parties. BCRA (often called McCain-Feingold after its Senate sponsors, Arizona Republican John McCain and Wisconsin Democrat Russ Feingold) also increased the limits for hard money—that is, direct contributions to campaigns. Individuals can now contribute $2,000 in primary

*John McCain (left) and Russ Feingold smile during a news conference about the McCain-Feingold campaign finance reform bill.*

elections and $2,000 in general elections for each individual candidate, up to a total of $37,500 over a two-year election cycle, as well as up to $25,000 to a national party and $10,000 each to state parties. Furthermore, BCRA provided that ads that refer to a federal candidate cannot be broadcast within thirty days of a primary and sixty days of an election.

It was not long, however, before wealthy donors and candidates figured out how to circumvent BCRA's soft money ban. This was done through the use of tax-exempt political organizations known as 527s, named after a provision of the U.S. tax code. These 527s function very similarly to political action committees (PACs), except that they are not regulated by the Federal Election Commission and are not limited in the amounts they can collect or spend for issue ads. As a result, 527 groups have proliferated. During the 2004 presidential election between President George W. Bush and Democratic senator John Kerry, for example, billionaire George Soros gave more than $23 million to liberal 527 groups such as the Media Fund and MoveOn.org, which ran ads criticizing President Bush. At the same time, a wealthy Houston home builder, Bob Perry, contributed more than $8 million to Swift Boat Veterans for Truth, a group that effectively mocked Kerry's previously respected Vietnam War record with a series of controversial, negative TV ads. Legislation has been introduced in both the House and the Senate to regulate 527s and similar political groups, but so far no new law has been enacted.

## Other U.S. Reform Proposals

Finding a perfect solution to the problem of campaign finance corruption, however, may not be possible. Most reform ideas center around one or more of just a few basic approaches—limiting campaign spending, limiting donations, disclosure of donations, providing public financing, or providing free TV time—many of which have proven flaws. Limits on campaign spending, for example, often run into constitutional challenges that they violate First Amendment free speech rights under *Buckley v. Valeo*. Legislative limits on donations and disclosure laws, as history has shown, tend to be easily circumvented by corporate and special interests determined to retain their influence on politics. The two remaining concepts—public funding and free TV airtime—now appear to be gaining more support.

In fact, a grassroots movement has been gaining ground in America to push for a public funding approach. This movement, called "Clean Money" or "Clean Elections," began in Maine in 1996, and has since mushroomed to six other states and two cities: Arizona; Connecticut; New Jersey; New Mexico; North Carolina; Vermont; Albuquerque, New Mexico; and Portland, Oregon. In November 2006, California voters failed to pass Proposition 89, which if approved would have authorized a Clean Money approach in that state. These laws differ somewhat from state to state but they all embody one simple idea—a voluntary public financing system to provide full public funding to state candidates in exchange for their agreement to limit their spending and not to take corporate and special-interest contributions.

# Clean Money Elections in Maine and Arizona

Maine and Arizona were the first two states to enact Clean Money initiatives to provide for public financing of state candidates. Maine voters approved the Maine Clean Election Act in 1996, and Arizona voters approved the Citizens Clean Elections Act two years later. In both states, the legislation was passed through citizen referendums rather than by the state legislatures, and later upheld by the state supreme courts after legal challenges. After several elections under these systems, advocates say the results are very positive. Most legislators currently serving in both states (80 percent of the current legislators in Maine

and ten out of eleven statewide officeholders in Arizona), for example, opted to use and were elected with public funds. The Clean Money system also produced more candidates, including many more women and minority candidates than in the past; allowed candidates to spend much more of their time interacting with voters; and increased voter turnout. Also, in recent years, legislators in both states have reportedly voted to protect the environment more often than before, have lowered the cost of prescription drugs, and have passed balanced budgets. These votes, advocates say, are the result of more representative governments.

Typically, the Clean Money laws weed out fringe candidates by providing that candidates wishing to receive public funding must be a nominee of a party recognized by the state. Secondly, candidates must qualify by collecting a set number of small individual contributions (usually around 250 donations of around five dollars each) from voters in their district. If they qualify, their campaigns are fully funded by the public and they are not permitted to use their own personal money or accept any outside donations, whether from individuals, corporations, or PACs. Candidates who choose not to participate in the Clean Money system can raise money from private donors, but they must follow state campaign finance limits and disclosure laws. If a Clean Money candidate faces an opponent who has chosen not to participate in the system and instead to accept large private contributions, most laws provide a matching grant, to a limit, to the publicly funded candidate. Extra funding is also often provided if the opposing candidate has the help of so-called independent groups, such as PACs and 527s.

Advocates of the Clean Money approach claim that it will clean up campaign finance corruption and promote better, more responsive government. By providing public campaign funds, they say, the program encourages a wider array of qualified candidates to run for office and eliminates some of the historical advantages held by incumbents. In addition, since candidates are freed from having to raise money for their campaigns, they are able to spend their campaign time discussing issues and interacting with voters. This leads to more substantive, issue-oriented elections and encourages the electorate to become more engaged in the political process. Finally, advocates argue that candidates who are elected with Clean Money will be better public servants, because they will not have to worry about fund-raising and will owe no favors to campaign contributors.

Similar legislation, called the Clean Money, Clean Elections Act (HR 3099), has been introduced in the House of Representatives by Massachusetts Democrat John Tierney and Arizona Democrat Raul Grijalva to provide full public funding for candidates running for the U.S. House of Representatives. Additionally, this bill would provide federal Clean Money candi-

## Clean Money Approach

Seven states and two cities now participate in the "Clean Elections" or "Clean Money" approach to reforming financial corruption in political campaigns.

dates with free or discounted TV broadcast time to help counter the effect of the other side's issue ads. HR 3099, however, has yet to garner widespread support, and like other reform ideas, it is not without criticism. Some commentators, for example, object to mandating free airtime because it would take profits away from private media companies. Others claim that public funding of campaigns forces taxpayers to make political donations and is simply welfare for politicians who otherwise could not get elect-ed. As libertarian political scientist John Samples argues: "Those who wish to support the candidates and causes favored by gov-ernment financing may do so now; they need only send their check to the candidate or cause they favor. Government financ-ing forces all taxpayers to financially support candidates they would not otherwise support, candidates whose views they may find repugnant."[51]

## Campaign Finance in Other Industrialized Countries

Other industrialized democratic countries face similar dilemmas about how to keep corporate and special-interest money from unduly influencing elections, but most do not experience any-where near the level of spending in the United States. Some of their solutions are similar to U.S. election finance reforms, such as the prohibition against corporations contributing directly to campaigns. In addition, contribution limits and public disclo-sure of private donations like the U.S. requirements are com-mon to most democracies.

### CORRUPTION HARD TO FIGHT

"Fighting corruption is not easy. Anti-corruption campaigns are more often limited to rhetoric [insincere discussion], and are only rarely sustained."

—Shang-Jin Wei, an economist and senior fellow at the
Brookings Institution, a private nonprofit public
policy research organization

Shang-Jin Wei, "Corruption and Globalization," Brookings Institution, April 2001. www.brook.edu/comm/policybriefs/pb79.htm.

However, many experts believe that most other democracies have had more success with campaign finance reform because they have adopted reforms that so far have been rejected or remain untried in the United States. For one thing, countries such as Canada, France, New Zealand, and Great Britain place strict limits on amounts candidates can spend on their campaigns—the type of spending limits ruled unconstitutional for America in *Buckley v. Valeo*. In Great Britain, for example, the spending limits are quite low and result in relatively inexpensive campaigns compared to the unlimited American campaign spending levels. As CNN correspondent Robin Oakley notes:

> Making a choice between John Kerry and George W. Bush cost some $1.2 billion. . . . Congressional elections boosted the bill to nearly $4 billion. Making a choice between these three men—Labor's Tony Blair, the conservative's Michael Howard and the Liberal Democrat's Charles Kennedy, with 646 members of the House of Commons thrown in on the deal—comes for little more than $18 million.[52]

In addition to spending limits, most foreign democracies have also adopted two other important reforms not yet widely used in the United States—public funding of elections and free TV airtime to candidates. Virtually all the northern European countries (Germany, France, Spain, Portugal, Ireland, Belgium, Austria, and the Netherlands) except for Great Britain, as well as Greece and Italy, for example, have adopted both these approaches in some form, along with Russia and most other countries in eastern Europe. Other countries embracing both public funding and free airtime include Switzerland, Canada, Australia, New Zealand, Israel, Argentina, Brazil, Costa Rica, and Mexico, as well as the Scandinavian countries (Denmark, Finland, Norway, and Sweden).

Yet these approaches have not necessarily rooted out all political corruption. As in the United States, political scandals continue to occur in Europe, despite the various anticorruption laws. In the end, therefore, reducing corruption may come down mostly to political will and enforcement efforts.

## Reason for Hope

The limited victories so far in the anticorruption campaign illustrate the difficulties involved with curbing corruption, whether on a local, national, or international level. Experts say future success will largely depend on the commitment of national governments around the world. This commitment, they say, will require not only the adoption of strong anticorruption measures (such as tranparency provisions, civil service reforms, and antibribery and campaign finance laws), but also the creation and funding of an effective central enforcement agency. Preventative actions, such as the adoption of laws to regulate corporate behavior and protect people who report corruption, will also be important. Achieving these goals will, in turn, depend on strong leadership, from both national and international leaders as well as the media, non-governmental organizations, and advocacy groups.

## PERKS OF THE POLITICAL CULTURE

"Congress won't change because it doesn't want to. Lawmakers like the perks of the sleazy inside-the-Beltway political culture—the private jets, the junkets, the ease with which they can line up contributions. And they're confident that if they posture long enough, the public and the media eventually will lose interest."
—*San Diego Union-Tribune*, a daily newspaper serving San Diego, California

*San Diego Union-Tribune,* "Reform Follies: Congress' Hollow Posturing Invites Cynicism," March 10, 2006.

Yet despite this huge task, anticorruption advocates say there is reason for hope, if only because giving in to such a negative force would be so damaging to everyone involved. As Ben Heineman Jr. and Fritz Heimann put it, "Ultimately, the most potent force for change is the idea that corruption is morally repugnant and inimical [adverse] to competition, globalization, the rule of law, international development, and the welfare of citizens around the world."[53]

## Chapter 1: The Problem of Political Corruption

1. International Monetary Fund, "Good Governance: The IMF's Role," August 1997, p. 2. www.imf.org/external/pubs/ft/exrp/govern/govern.pdf#search=%22the%20abuse%20of%20public%20office%20for%20private%20gain%201997%20World%20Bank%22.

2. Steven P. Lanza, "The Economics of Ethics: The Cost of Political Corruption," *Connecticut Economy Quarterly*, February 24, 2004. http://ccea.uconn.edu/studies/The%20Economics%20of%20Ethics-%20The%20Cost%20of%20Political%20Corruption.pdf.

3. Susan Rose-Ackerman, *Government and Corruption: Causes, Consequences, and Reform*. New York: Cambridge University Press, 1999, p. 113.

4. Quoted in Barbara Crossette, "Corruption's Threat to Democracy," *Atlantic Online,* April 12, 2004. www.theatlantic.com/foreign/unwire/crossette2004-04-12.htm.

5. Rose-Ackerman, *Government and Corruption*, p. 132.

6. Elizabeth Drew, *The Corruption of American Politics: What Went Wrong and Why*. New York: Overlook, 1999, p. 64.

7. Stephen Lendman, "Democracy in America—It's Spelled C-O-R-R-U-P-T-I-O-N," Countercurrents.org, February 16, 2006. www.countercurrents.org/us-lendman130206.htm.

8. Shang-Jin Wei, "Corruption in Economic Development: Beneficial Grease, Minor Annoyance, or Major Obstacle?" World Bank. www.worldbank.org/wbi/governance/pdf/wei.pdf.

9. Nancy Zucker Boswell and Peter Richardson, "Anti-corruption: Unshackling Economic Development," *Economic Perspectives,*

March 2003. http://usinfo.state.gov/journals/ites/0303/ijee/bos well.htm.

## Chapter 2: Political Corruption in America

10. Quoted in Nathan Miller, *Stealing from America: A History of Corruption from Jamestown to Reagan*. St. Paul, MN: Paragon House, 1992, p. 167.

11. Quoted in Steve Padilla, "In Politics, Money Talks—and Keeps Talking, Despite Reforms," *Los Angeles Times*, July 16, 2000. www.campaignfinancesite.org/history/reform3.html.

12. Miller, *Stealing from America*, p. 262.

13. Frank J. Sorauf, *Money in American Elections*. Glenview, IL: Scott, Foresman, 1988, p. 32.

14. Sorauf, *Money in American Elections*, pp. 34–35.

15. Miller, *Stealing from America*, p. 307.

16. Drew, *The Corruption of American Politics*, p. 39.

## Chapter 3: Money and Political Corruption in the United States

17. Mark Green, *Selling Out: How Big Corporate Money Buys Elections, Rams Through Legislation, and Betrays Our Democracy*. New York: Regan, 2002, p. 4. www.thirdworld traveler.comElection_Reform/Campaigning_Money_SO. html.

18. Green, *Selling Out*, p. 105.

19. Green, *Selling Out*, p. 107.

20. Quoted in Mollie Dickenson, "John McCain: Straight Shooter?" *Consortium News*, 2000. www.consortiumnews.com/2000/012 900b.html.

21. Miller, *Stealing from America*, p. 341.

22. Miller, *Stealing from America*, p. 341.

23. Kevin Phillips, "Dynasties," *Nation*, July 8, 2002. www.the nation.com/doc/20020708/phillips.

24. John Nichols, "Enron: What Dick Cheney Knew," *Nation*, April 15, 2002. www.thenation.com/doc/20020415/nichols.

25. Nichols, "Enron."

26. Quoted in Tim Wheeler, "Enron Entangles Bush, Cheney," *People's Weekly World*, June 1, 2002. www.pww.org/article/view/1297/1/88/.

27. Sam Parry, "Bush and Ken Lay: Slip Slidin' Away," *Consortium News*, February 6, 2002. www.consortiumnews.com/2002/020602a1.html.

28. Bill Moyers, "A Culture of Corruption," *Washington Spectator*, April 1, 2006. www.truthout.org/docs_2006/040806G.shtml.

**Chapter 4: Political Corruption Around the World**

29. Robert Klitgaard, "International Cooperation Against Corruption," Internet Center for Corruption Research, November 1997. www.icgg.org/downloads/contribution02_klitgaard.pdf.

30. Quoted in Roshan Muhammed Salih, "Poor Nations Found to Be Most Corrupt," Al Jazeera, October 20, 2004. http://english.aljazeera.net/NR/exeres/DBFAB979-5B46-44AC-AA34-A4D948A8219F.htm.

31. Kimberly Ann Elliott, ed., *Corruption and the Global Economy*. Washington, DC: Institute for International Economics, 1997, p. 2.

32. Quoted in United Nations Department of Public Information, "The Cost of Corruption," February 2000. www.un.org/events/10thcongress/2088b.htm.

33. Shang-Jin Wei, "Corruption and Globalization," Brookings Institution, April 2001. www.brook.edu/comm/policybriefs/pb79.htm.

34. Quoted in Tanja Subotic and Banja Luka, "'Nothing Can Be Done Without Corruption' in Bosnia," *Mail & Guardian Online*, January 2006. www.mg.co.za/articlePage.aspx?articleid=260107&area=/ insight/insight__international/.

35. Elliott, *Corruption and the Global Economy*, pp. 1–2.

36. Drew, *The Corruption of American Politics*, p. viii.

37. Robert Neild, *Public Corruption: The Dark Side of Social Evolution*. London: Anthem, 2002, p. 209.

38. Susan Hawley, *Exporting Corruption: Privatisation, Multi-nationals and Bribery*. Dorset, UK: Corner House, June 2000. www.thecornerhouse.org.uk/pdf/briefing/19bribe.pdf.

39. Hawley, *Exporting Corruption*.

40. Patrick Glynn, Stephen J. Kobrin, and Moisés Naím, "The Globalization of Corruption," *Corruption and the Global Economy*, p. 13.

## Chapter 5: Efforts to Curb Political Corruption

41. Glynn, Kobrin, and Naím, "The Globalization of Corruption," p. 9.

42. Neild, *Public Corruption*, pp. 136–37.

43. Glynn, Kobrin, and Naím, "The Globalization of Corruption," p. 10.

44. Quoted in Mario Ritter, "The World Bank Fights the 'Cancer of Corruption,'" *Voice of America*, April 7, 2006. www.voanews.com/specialenglish/archive/2006-04/2006-04-07voa 2.cfm.

45. Ben W. Heineman Jr. and Fritz Heimann, "The Long War Against Corruption," *Foreign Affairs*, May/June 2006. www.foreignaffairs.org/20060501faessay85305/ben-w-heineman-jr-fritz-heimann/the-long-war- against-corruption.html.

46. John Brademas and Fritz Heimann, "Tackling International Corruption: No Longer Taboo," *Foreign Affairs*, September/October 1998. www.foreignaffairs.org/19980901facomment 1414/john-brademas-fritz-heimann/tackling-international-corruption-no-longer-taboo.html.

47. Quoted in Donald Greenlees, "Anti-corruption Fight Stalled," *International Herald Tribune*, May 31, 2006. http://66.102. 7.104/search?q=cache:Hc8zWgQf4usJ:www.iht.com/articles/2006/04/05/business/corrupt.php+developing+countries+anticorruption+reforms+2006&hl=en&gl=us&ct=clnk&cd=2.

48. Quoted in United States House of Representatives, "Christopher Shays and Marty Meehan, testimony before the House Administration Committee On H.R. 417, the Bipartisan Cam-

paign Finance Reform Act," June 29, 1999. www.house.gov/ shays/reform/ 629test5.htm.

49. Darrell M. West, *Checkbook Democracy: How Money Corrupts Political Campaigns.* Boston: Northeastern University Press, 2000, p. 167.

50. West, *Checkbook Democracy*, p. 170.

51. John Samples, ed., *Welfare for Politicians: Taxpayer Financing of Campaigns.* Washington, DC: Cato Institute, 2005, p. 17.

52. Quoted in CNN.com, "Transcripts: Judy Woodruff's Inside Politics," May 2, 2005. http://transcripts.cnn.com/TRAN SCRIPTS/0505/02/ ip.01.html.

53. Heineman and Heimann, "The Long War Against Corruption."

## Chapter 1: The Problem of Political Corruption

1. What does the term *political corruption* mean, according to the definition used by international organizations?
2. What is the relationship between corruption and democracy, according to the author?
3. What are some of the most common forms of corruption in developing countries? For more developed nations?

## Chapter 2: Political Corruption in America

1. What U.S. law first prohibited corporations and banks from contributing directly to political campaigns?
2. According to the book, why were the 1974 FECA amendments unsuccessful in stopping the flow of corporate money into elections?
3. What do the terms *bundling* and *soft money* mean?

## Chapter 3: Money and Political Corruption in the United States

1. Why are American presidential and congressional campaigns so expensive, according to the author?
2. What are some of the effects of the role of money in American politics?
3. Describe some of the presidential, congressional, and corporate corruption scandals in recent American history.

## Chapter 4: Political Corruption Around the World

1. According to information presented by the author, what developing countries or regions have the highest levels of political corruption?
2. Why is corruption especially harmful to developing countries?

3. What effect has globalization had on corruption, according to the author?

## Chapter 5: Efforts to Curb Political Corruption

1. Why is there an increased focus on corruption today, according to the book?
2. Describe some of the efforts that have been taken at the international level to reform problems of corruption and explain how effective they have been so far.
3. How do the Clean Money/Clean Elections laws work to combat the problem of money in American elections?

**ORGANIZATIONS TO CONTACT**

**The Brookings Institution**
1775 Massachusetts Ave. NW
Washington, DC 20036
(202) 797-6000
Web site: www.brook.edu/

The Brookings Institution is a private, nonprofit research organization that provides analysis and recommendations for policy makers on a wide range of public policy issues. Its Web site contains an informative category on U.S. politics and campaign finance reform, with links to a number of Brookings publications on the topic.

**The Center for Responsive Politics (CRP)**
1101 Fourteenth St. NW, Suite 1030
Washington, DC 20005-5635
(202) 857-0044 • fax (202) 857-7809
Web site: www.crp.org/index.asp

The CRP is a nonpartisan, nonprofit research group that tracks money in politics and its effect on elections and public policy. The center conducts computer-based research on campaign finance issues for the news media, academics, activists, and the public at large. Its Web site contains numerous up-to-date articles about campaign finance in the United States.

**Citizens for Responsibility and Ethics in Washington (CREW)**
1400 Eye St. NW, Suite 450
Washington, DC 20005
(202) 408-5565
Web site: www.citizensforethics.org/

CREW is a legal advocacy group that targets corrupt government officials and uses litigation and public advocacy to expose corrupt activities. The CREW Web site contains information about corruption scandals and the group's various legal actions.

## Common Cause

1133 Nineteenth St. NW, 9th Floor
Washington, DC 20036
(202) 833-1200
Web site: www.commoncause.org/

Common Cause is a nonpartisan, nonprofit advocacy organization founded in 1970 by John Gardner to encourage citizen participation in democracy and to promote an honest, open, and accountable government. It has almost three hundred thousand members and supporters and offices in thirty-eight states. Its Web site contains a wealth of information about money in U.S. politics and anticorruption reforms.

## Corner House

Station Rd., Sturminster Newton
Dorset DT10 1YJ, UK
+44 (0)1258 473795 • fax: +44 (0)1258 473748
Web site: www.thecornerhouse.org.uk

The Corner House is a nonprofit British charity that conducts analysis, research, and advocacy aimed at supporting democratic and community movements for environmental and social justice. Its Web site provides links to many studies and publications relating to the topic of international anticorruption efforts.

## Federal Election Commission (FEC)

999 E St. NW
Washington, DC 20463
(800) 424-9530
Web site: www.fec.gov

The U.S. Congress created the FEC as an independent agency in 1975 to administer and enforce the Federal Election Campaign Act, the statute that governs the financing of federal elections. The duties of the FEC are to disclose campaign finance information, to enforce the provisions of the law such as the limits and prohibitions on contributions, and to oversee the public funding of presidential elections. The FEC Web site provides information about campaign finance laws and enforcement efforts.

**Transparency International–USA (TI–USA)**
1023 Fifteenth St. NW, Suite 300
Washington, DC 20005
(202) 589-1616 • fax: (202) 589-1512
Web site: www.transparency-usa.org/

Transparency International (TI) is a Berlin-based nonprofit, nonpartisan organization founded in 1993 to curb corruption in international trade and transactions. TI has chapters in over eighty countries, including the United States. It encourages governments to implement effective anticorruption laws and policies, promotes reform through international organizations, and raises public awareness. Its U.S. Web site contains a link to the main TI Web site as well as a long list of publications on the topic of corruption.

# FOR MORE INFORMATION

## Books

Elizabeth Drew, *The Corruption of American Politics: What Went Wrong and Why*. New York: Overlook, 1999. A readable account of how money has changed American politics over the past several decades.

Mark Green, *Selling Out: How Big Corporate Money Buys Elections, Rams Through Legislation, and Betrays Our Democracy*. New York: Regan, 2002. An indictment of the influence of corporate money in American politics, forcefully argued.

Jim Hightower, *Thieves in High Places: They've Stolen Our Country—and It's Time to Take It Back*. New York: Viking, 2003. An entertaining and unscholarly look at how elites are running Congress and stealing U.S. democracy, by a national radio commentator and writer.

Arianna Huffington, *Pigs at the Trough: How Corporate Greed and Political Corruption Are Undermining America*. New York: Crown, 2003. A readable and opinionated book about the alliance between politicians, lobbyists, and corporations in America.

Bertram I. Spector, *Fighting Corruption in Developing Countries: Strategies and Analysis*. Bloomfield, CT: Kumarian, 2005. A scholarly look at corruption in developing countries, analyzed according to nine sectors: education, agriculture, energy, environment, health, justice, private business, political parties, and public finance.

## Periodicals

John Brademas and Fritz Heimann, "Tackling International Corruption: No Longer Taboo," *Foreign Affairs*, September/October 1998.

Silla Brush and Edward T. Pound, "Who's Sorry Now?" *U.S. News & World Report*, December 12, 2005.

James Carville and Paul Begala, "Not One Dime: A Radical Plan to Abramoff-Proof Politics," *Washington Monthly*, March 2006.

Thomas L. Friedman, "The First Law of Petropolitics," *Foreign Policy*, May/June 2006.

Ben W. Heineman Jr. and Fritz Heimann, "The Long War Against Corruption," *Foreign Affairs*, May/June 2006.

Mark Schmitt, "The Limits of Limits," *American Prospect*, March 2006.

Patrick Tucker, "Fighting Corruption in Developing Nations," *Futurist*, January–February 2006.

## Web sites

**Anticorruption, World Bank** (web.worldbank.org/WEBSITE/ EXTERNAL/TOPICS/EXTPUBLICSECTORANDGOVER NANCE/EXTANTICORRUPTION/0,,menuPK:384461~pageP K:149018~piPK:149093~theSitePK:384455,00.html). A Web site that describes the World Bank's strategies for combating corruption in various developing countries.

**Campaign Finance: Special Report, Washington Post.com** (www.washingtonpost.com/wp-srv/politics/special/campfin/ campfin.htm). A media Web site on campaign finance that provides a useful overview of the subject, along with links to *Washington Post* articles and anticorruption organizations.

**Clean Money Clean Elections Public Campaign, Public Campaign Action Fund** (www.publicampaign.org/clean-facts). A national Web site organized to provide information and advocate for the Clean Money approach to campaign financing, with a good overview and links to state Clean Money campaigns.

**Corruption, Organization for Economic Cooperation and Development** (www.oecd.org/topic/0,2686,en_2649_37447 _1_1_1_1_37447,00.html). A Web site that provides detailed information about the Organization for Economic Cooperation and Development's efforts to prevent international bribery and corruption.

**Corruption Perceptions Index, Transparency International** (www. transparency.org/policy_research/surveys_indices/cpi). A ranking of more than 150 countries by their perceived levels of corruption, as determined by expert assessments and opinion surveys.

# INDEX

# PICTURE CREDITS

Cover photo: © Bettmann/Corbis
Maury Aaseng, 16, 82, 89
AP Images, 9, 15, 17, 52, 66
Sabah Arar/AFP/Getty Images, 74
Terry Ashe/Getty Images, 37
Gustavo Benitez/AFP/Getty Images, 64, 70 (main photo)
Adek Berry/AFP/Getty Images, 61
© Bettmann/Corbis, 28, 33, 50
Karen Bleier/AFP/Getty Images, 20
© Corbis, 28, 29, 31
Getty Images, 70 (inset)
Chris Hondros/Newsmakers/Getty Images, 45
Sandy Huffaker/Getty Images, 7
Michael Kleinfeld/Landov, 65
The Library of Congress, 27
© B. Marthur/Reuters/Corbis, 51
© Gabe Palmer/zefa/Corbis, 77
© Reuters/Corbis, 55
Paul J. Richards/AFP/Getty Images, 39, 57
George Silk, Time Life Pictures/Getty Images, 35
Andreas Solaro/AFP/Getty Images, 65
Diana Walker/Time and Life Pictures/Getty Images, 49
Alex Wong/Newsmakers/Getty Images, 80, 85

# ABOUT THE AUTHOR

Debra A. Miller is a writer and lawyer with a passion for current events and history. She began her law career in Washington, D.C., where she worked on legislative, policy, and legal matters in government, public interest, and private law firm positions. She now lives with her husband in Encinitas, California. She has written and edited numerous books and anthologies on historical and political topics.